Autobiography
of
CHARLES A. JONES

FRANCES CHERMANSKY

Fulton Books, Inc.
Meadville, PA

Published by Fulton Books 2021

ISBN 978-1-63860-662-8 (paperback)
ISBN 978-1-63860-663-5 (digital)

Printed in the United States of America

Arch has a winner! He did a marvelous autobiography. It's factual, truthful, interesting, enjoyable & entertaining! We always admired his drive and "Can Do" spirit. To tackle a book, and do so well at in his 90's, or at any age for that matter, deserves much acclimation.

Thank you for letting us read it.

Joan Wilson Vernon & Enola Wilson

May 17, 1910

I WAS BORN AT Weisel Corners, a farm on the corner of Salts Springs and Lyntz Roads in Lordstown. The first thing I can remember was around 1913 or 1914. We were living on a farm on Palmyra Road (the first farm west of Lordstown Township at Duck Creek) with our old friend and neighbor of many years. His name was I. B. Wood, and he was a civil war veteran. He was like an uncle to our family. My clearest recollection was of me sitting on his shoulders, and I was cutting his hair. Of course, my mom was furious, but Mr. Wood told her that he was enjoying me cutting his hair.

Arthur and Edna Pearl Jones and son Charles Archer Jones

Then we lived in Newton Falls for about three months with my grandmother Jones. She had what they called a small-time hotel and/or boarding house. At this time, they were building a streetcar line from Youngstown, Warren, Newton Falls to Alliance and beyond. It took a lot of men, horses, etc., to build it, so the eating and sleeping places did well in that area for a couple of years. We lived on Canal Street across from the jail and fire station. The fire equipment at that time was a wagon filled with fire hose which they plugged into a couple of fire plugs, in and near the center of town, getting pressure from hand-pumped cisterns and wells. The wagon was pulled by four to six men. They later built a theater where the hotel was originally.

The next thing that I remember we had moved to Windham, Ohio. I think we moved on account of my dad's job. He worked for the Rawleigh Company, and his territory was in that area. Dad had a two-horse vehicle that looked like an Amish buggy, only quite a lot larger. One was a black horse named Bell and the other was a sorrel with a white face. Bell had a colt that won a blue ribbon, and Bell won a white ribbon for best driving horse class at the Trumbull County Fair. Dad was a good horseman.

Dad and his Raleigh wagon

One thing that stands out in my mind was my grandpa Jones came to visit one evening and it was the first time I can remember seeing him.

And one day, a man came who was dressed and looked like Buffalo Bill. He had a gun in a holster, long hair, and a beard and looked like Bill's twin. Actually, he was a US marshal from California who came to visit his brother who was hanging wallpaper at our house. As young as I was, it was one of the big thrills of my life.

Next, we moved to the Sherman farm in Newton Falls Township. My brother, Floyd, was born there on May 25, 1915. While we lived there, I stepped on a rusty nail and got a case of blood poisoning and had a bad time for a while. About the fall of 1916, I got to go to school for about one month at the old one-room schoolhouse. It was located about a quarter mile west of our place. Eunice Evans was the teacher of all grades. There were eighteen pupils from first to eighth grade. There was only one student in the eighth grade. Then we moved to Warren where I started again in the first grade at Dickey Avenue School. The teacher was Ms. Booth and the principal was Ms. Andrews. We lived on Ward Avenue between Oregon and Nevada Streets. I went to Dickey Avenue School for three years.

While we lived there, my brother Burt and I had a few little episodes. We sold candy to residents in the area at Christmastime for the Watkins Products Co. My aunt, Edna Piltz, was the agent for them. We earned enough coupons to get us each an Ingersol watch. Cost at that time was one dollar. I had my first experience going to a store by myself. Rowlands grocery was a two-story wooden building at the corner of Market and Parkman Road. Well, Mom gave me a nickel to buy candy, plus the grocery money. Well, I had no experience with money before, so I really felt like a big spender and tried to get three of everything that was displayed in the candy case. Finally Mr. Rowland asked me how much money I was to spend on candy, and I proudly showed him the nickel.

Well, he already had about fifty cents worth in a bag, so he removed about half of the candy and let me take the rest home. There was a candy factory at the corner of Haymaker Street and Market Street with the City Lumber Yard next to it. Burt and I were walking on Market Street toward town from Oregon Street and saw a big cloud of smoke ahead of us and saw a fire pump and hose wagon, pulled by a team of horses coming from the fire department on Franklin Street—one of the last horse-drawn pieces before motorized equipment in Warren. Dad bought the first family automobile in 1917; it was either a 1913 or 1914 Model T Ford with only a crank start, no battery.

A friend on the left, myself on the right

Then we moved again to IB Wood farm in the spring. I was nine years old and should have started in the fourth grade, but due to the difference in school standards, they put me back in the third grade in the new school. In Newton Falls, the third and fourth grades went across from the main school which was on School Street. We lived about four miles from the school, but six miles if we rode around the block, which was a mile square. There were four farms in the square mile, and we lived on the southeast corner.

The Yeager farm joined the Wood farm on the north. Mr. Yeager died from one of the common ailments of those times: blood poisoning. That was before penicillin was discovered. He passed away leaving six children, all boys, the oldest was fourteen years old and the youngest was under a year. The mother continued with that big farm of 175 acres for several years with very little help except for those six boys. My brother Burt and I spent many hours trying to help them with their many chores and also played in the little leisure time they had. Sunday was set aside for rest and play. Burt and I and three or four of the Yeager boys, most warm summer Sundays, took off for the wooded areas and looked for weasel or skunk dens. They both were farm pests that raided the chicken coops, stealing eggs and killing any kind of fowl. Yeagers had an ice house, and Burt and I helped the boys to fill it by cutting ice from a pond on the Wood farm. We used a one-man crosscut saw to cut the blocks about one to one and a half by three feet.

Sometimes when we were done cutting, we decided to play tag by jumping from one piece of floating ice to another. But one day, we got in bad trouble. Burt slipped and fell under the floating ice, and the rest of us boys had an awful hard time getting him out. We all got soaked and had to go to the house and get dried out. No one caught cold, but you can be sure that ended the tag game on floating ice! The winters were different then than now; it would freeze ice thick enough in November to skate on, and even most running streams and ponds would freeze real deep. Not anymore.

When the folks would go away and the Yeager boys were with us, about two or three of them, Burt and I would get broom sticks and go up the attic and invade the bats that were always numerous in the spaces between the nailing strips under the slates on the roof. Of course, us boys would usually get a few red marks from one another's poor marksmanship and wild swings. Well, we got hit when the folks got home and saw the swollen ears and many other marks of our battle with the bats!

Our cousin Jessie Piltz, Burt, and I ice-skated from our house to the railroad underpass in Leavittsburg on Thanksgiving Day in 1920.

I saw a great many hobos that came from the railroad which ran parallel with our barnyard fence. There was a well and a water trough where we had an old iron pump. My brother Burt and I spent many hours playing with that old pump. We also helped Dad while we were having fun. At the pump was where we would meet the hobos when they would stop to get a drink. I don't ever remember anyone who was not nice and kind to us. My mother was kind and would give us sandwiches to give them. Some of them would stay over with us for a day or so and help Dad with the farmwork. They would sleep in the barn while they were with us. If they were clean, Mom would let them have the evening meal in the house with us; otherwise, they ate outside. Sometimes we would get up in the morning and our guests would be gone, but most would tell Dad the evening before that they were leaving in the morning.

We moved from the Wood farm to Leavittsburg for about four months before moving to Warren. The house was within arm's reach of the streetcar tracks which ran on south side of four sets of railroad tracks. It was quite an interesting but noisy place. Of course, I only went to school there a short while, and I have very few fond memories of that place.

In 1920, we moved to Parkman Road in Warren on the east side between Maxwell Avenue and Niblock Avenue. Parkman Road at that time was unpaved. Until 1922, we still had Buster, our pony. At that time, Niblock was the north side of city limits. The street was black cinders into Summit Street, which was brick with streetcar tracks running from Ohio Street to Mahoning Avenue and south to downtown Warren.

I entered Dickey Avenue School, and they put me in the sixth grade, skipping the fifth on account of the difference in school ratings. I missed being in the fifth grade, so I was back on track again and happy about it. That's where I acquired the nickname Archie the Cop or just Cop, taken from the comic strip in the daily newspaper.

My grandpa Jones was back living with us again after leaving us when we moved from the Sherman farm. He worked at the Borden machine shop, later the Beaver Pipe and Tool. They paid the workers weekly with all of ten dollars and over in gold until 1923. Grandpa had purchased two lots on Maxwell and two on Niblock Avenue, end to end, which about one hundred feet from back of our lot. So that became the neighborhood playground and ball field. Us kids in the area spent a lot of time there, but we also went fishing on the Mahoning River and wandering through the wood area in back of our place. It is now all built up with houses. I had several special friends from there that I kept in touch with for many years after we moved from Warren: Charles Walton (Ducky), Earl Swartz (Jake), Lee St. Clair (Deeno), Robert Maxwell (Bob), and Langford Maxwell (Lanky).

Ducky and I played more baseball than any of the others. We played with men on church teams at Packard Park and Perkins Park. They were usually short of players, who had to work overtime. There was always an opening for us on nice summer evenings.

I went from Dickey Avenue School to West Junior School on Palmyra Road in the seventh grade. It was one of the first junior high schools in Warren. Ms. Fletcher was the principal. I went there through the eighth grade.

Then in the fall of 1924, we moved to Hollywood Avenue, east of Elm Road. During my tenth to fifteenth year living in Warren, I spent some of my summer and vacation times with the Kuntz family in Paris Township in Portage County. Uncle George and Aunt Leuella and cousins Clementine, Herald, Glen, and Russell. We did farm chores, baseball, tag in the barn on rainy days. In early fall, when green apples would fall, and a few that did not fall, naturally, we put them on a twig about three feet long and fling them as far as two hundred feet. And at times, we played war with them which was not a very bright thing to do. They would smart like hell if we got hit by them. We also followed after the plow when they were plowing and looked for arrowheads which were plentiful in that area. Likely it was the site of a bygone Indian village. It must have been a village as we found a lot of flint pieces also.

Then in 1925, we moved to a farm in Lordstown on the corner of Ernest Lyntz and Warren Road. The summer before, or early fall while at Kuntz's, I had my first job away from home. It was hauling water with horses and a tank wagon from the nearest well, pond, creek, etc. I hauled the water to a thrashing machine wherever needed on farms within a ten-mile radius of Paris Township. Sometimes we would be too far from Mr. Fackler's home to get back after work, so we slept wherever we were, sometimes in the homes where we were thrashing if they had room, but most nights we slept in their barns. The boss, Frank Fackler, and his wife were very old-fashioned farmers. Their work hours were long; we started before daylight and ended after dark. I was paid two dollars a day and room and board for six days. Oh boy, $12 a week was big-time money for me at the age of fourteen; farmhands were getting $30 a month and room and board on average.

Schooltime in the fall, so back to my home again. Earlier that summer, my cousins and I did most all the farmwork with playtime in the evenings and rainy days. My uncle was a baseball fan, and a couple of times that summer, he took us to Cleveland to see the Indians. The games were played at Euclid Park, and the outfield fence was along the sidewalk on Euclid Avenue. The fence was made of wooden planks. We got to see the Yanks play, and Babe Ruth hit two home runs and a foul ball over the right field wall. A real thrill for us boys. Tris Speaker was also playing.

In October of 1925, we moved to Lordstown. I was late starting school that year. So that kind of gave me a slow start on some of the subjects such as algebra, which I never did catch on to, but I did get good grades in everything except music and that damned algebra. I had a good year in baseball and basketball. We did not have enough boys in high school to make up a football team. We lived four miles from the school, and we played all competition games after school hours. With no way to go home and back in time to play, I had to stay at or near the school. Of course, in those times, our school transportation was horses and wagons or walking. By the next year or so, they started to get buses.

I did a very dumb thing after that year and never went back to school again. And I have paid the price for quitting school after only nine years ever since. If you ever have the misfortune to read this mixed-up mess, you will understand why.

I always loved the farm life, mud roads, and animals with the freedom and beauty of the outdoor living. I always loved horses and dogs the most, but I like all the rest of nature's beasts, even most humans. I've been writing this on an electric typewriter and having a hell of a hard time trying to control the critter. It just gets out of hand misspelling and all sorts of crazy things. I guess progress has passed me up a long time ago. So I struggle onward!

The first summer we were on the farm, my father let me use one-fourth acre of new ground. I had my first project of my own to work on. I cleaned the henhouse, pigpen, barn, and any other places that I could find fertilizer. I hauled it to my garden and made a lot of hills for watermelon, cantaloupe, and cucumbers and had several rows of corn and potatoes, plus a patch of turnips. We also had a large garden near the house that I kept up that summer. We had an overabundance of vegetables, but there was not very much fruit on the farm. There was one cherry and one plum tree, but Dad planted several fruit trees later on.

After school was out, I started to work with my dad in the summer of 1927 as an apprentice carpenter. I had to join the carpenters' union. I made $10 a week for six days of work for the first year, then it raised to $22 a week in 1928.

I bought my first car, a 1923 Chevrolet—three hundred dollars' worth of trouble, but an interesting possession. I had my first real experience with the workings of motor vehicles. I found out that the darn things were not nearly as smart as horses. They did not know gee from haw. It took awhile for me to get used to the brute. It had a hole in the floor with just a tin cover that slid over to let your hand through to the flywheel that the clutch ran inside of. The clutch had leather facing.

1927 was the year that I got my dog, Ted, which was one of the smartest animals I can ever remember seeing. He was a mostly German shepherd with tan legs and a black body. A real beauty. Ted looked after my baby sister, Ilene, who was a cute two-year-old then. He would take her wrist in his mouth very gently and take her to the neighbor's house across the road. He always stopped to see if there were any cars on the road; if he could see one, he would hold her back. The secondary roads were still dirt at that time, and we only had two or three cars pass our place in a day.

I got my model T Ford that summer. I traded my Chevy for it even up. I don't know why, but my uncle George Kuntz asked me if I would trade him cars, so I made the trade. He said he would paint the Ford for me as part of the deal if I would buy the paint, so I went to a Ford dealer and got a quart of Ford's only color. It cost $1. So I had a shiny car and a really enjoyed it until 1929 when I bought a 1927 Chevy. It was just a year before the whole country went bottom side up.

But we still had work for that year. Then things got tough. In 1930, I earned $700. I was married to Alice May King, the girl that I had went with for two years when I was nineteen years old and she was eighteen. Betty Jean was born May 22, 1929, and Bob was born May 22, 1930. I just can't say anything but nice things about the years we had together until we separated.

We built a little house on Bailey Road. At that time, the road was one side dirt and one side was improved by slag from Lyntz Road to Bailey's corner. (There was a political story about the oddity of that road later if I have time.) We got frame lumber from Alice's father and bought the rest from East Ohio Lumber Co. for $675, all but the roof shingles. I bought one-half acre of land for $150 and built a chicken coop and, later, a large corncrib. We had a couple of years until the Depression really hit hard; almost everybody in this country got hit. I worked in my father in-law's sawmill in the '20s and '30s to pay for the lumber he furnished for the little house Alice and I built. I hauled logs from places where they scattered around the mill yard and put them in position to be sawed. In the winter, it was real cold and oftentimes the logs were frozen to the ground and were difficult to get loose.

One morning, I hooked the tongs into a big old log that was frozen to the ground and extra hard to get loose. The horses were straining to pull it out when one of the big black horses named Dewey sunk his front legs through the frozen sod up to his shoulders in a sinkhole, and we had to hook the other horse to him to pull him out. There were a great many of those sinkholes in that area in those years. They weren't usually known about until some poor critter got caught in one. They were just pockets of quicksand from two and a half feet to forty feet across. The largest one that I saw was in our pasture; it had a rail fence around it when Dad bought the farm in 1925. We cut a few trees, and Dad had the stumps blown out. Burt and I hauled the stumps and brush that we cut along fence rows and filled it in. It was about fourteen feet deep in the center. Most folks filled them with rock and dirt; we used dirt and miscellaneous stuff we hauled home from buildings that Dad built.

Another crazy thing I remember doing: I had this big Belgian mare that needed a new collar as the one I had was in bad condition, so my neighbor Warren Trimbath and I started out one morning to try to pick up a good used one. A lot of the farmers had started to get tractors, which were taking the place of horses in the early twenties. Well, we found many horse collars, but none large enough, as Bessie took a size 24. So rather than wasting a day's walking, Warren decided to buy an old gray horse for $10. After walking about five miles leading a horse, we found a good size 24 horse collar for just $1 about half mile from our house in the opposite direction we had walked all day. That was in the tough years, but we both laughed about it later on.

Me and Alice
Bob and Betty

In 1931, I only got a couple of days' work at repair jobs and a few days' farmwork. At haymaking and thrashing time, I averaged $1.50 a day. In 1932, I sold a heifer that I had raised on the home farm and bought a horse from a man who had too many horses and not enough feed. So I bought the horse very cheap. The Stitle brothers that I had known and worked for when they needed help had an extra horse they loaned to me until I could buy another horse by trading labor for it. I borrowed money later on from the same brothers, Charlie and Emery Stitle, two real good friends. Horses and dogs have always been my two favorite animals, but I like most all of earth's creatures. Oh, there a few that I'm not real fond of, such as fire ants.

The year 1932 was a big year for me! I had no job; there just were no jobs of any kind available anywhere. So it was a real hard life trying to get enough money to pay for bare necessities of life. I took over the home farm on shares with Dad, and Dad rented the house to a family from New York to get money to pay on the taxes and mortgage.

I worked days now and then for other farmers for whatever they could pay. Very little money, mostly young pigs, a calf, chickens and even eggs, fruit and produce. It was hard for most everyone.

I had my tonsils taken out in Dr. McCaughtry's home, lying on a bay window seat on Sunday morning. Doc said it was a must. I had a lot of throat problems then. I sold some produce and a couple of chickens to pay for the anesthetic, and Doc took thirty-five baskets of corn for his surgical fee. It cost $35 for surgery and $8 for the anesthetic. Doc's wife was a nurse, and her care was free. They were all very kind people.

I had the car yet, but no money for license or gas. It still had its original tires and battery. I kept the tires inflated, but the battery was dead. My real estate taxes were due along with the mortgage payments, so I decided to sell the car. But I could not find a buyer. So I felt like a man standing on a hangman's platform, ready to be hung. So I went to a junkyard in Warren, which was the only place I was told was doing any auto business. They, of course, sold car parts at prices that were low enough that people could afford at that time. Well, the first place I went offered me $10. I guess they saw tears in my eyes, so they upped it to $12.50. Well, that sure was a hell of a discouraging day, but there were many more to follow.

I raised some wheat and took it over to the Phalanx grist mill and traded it for flour, and Alice was a good baker, so she baked seven or eight loaves of bread twice each week. She sold it to the neighbors for .10 cents a loaf. Whoa!

I also worked at the in-law's sawmill to pay for the framing lumber for the house and buildings. I hauled logs for the neighbors, and I also cut and hauled some of the last chestnut trees that grew in this area. All the timbers used in the Quimby Park shelter house came from there. I worked for the Stitle Brothers for $1.50 and .25 cents and supper if and when they needed me to help with evening chores. I also ran transit level for several thousand feet of field tile. My neighbor, Warren Trimbath, and I made apple sauce one fall. The Stitle brothers gave us apples. Warren and I picked them, and Emery Stitle helped to peel them and cook them in a ten-gallon copper kettle. Charlie furnished the apple gel and other spices, and we divided it three ways. We made about twenty-five gallons and sold it for a few dollars apiece. We also had large gardens at home where we raised potatoes, cabbage, tomatoes, peppers, etc., and pedaled it from house to house. The cabbage sold for 1.5 cents a pound, potatoes .75 cents to $1 a bushel, cauliflower .05 cents to .15 cents. I remember that at the butcher shop they gave 1 pound of liver free with 1 pound of steak.

I had a lifelong friend, Charlie Sheldon, who was also a neighbor since we moved to Lordstown. We helped each other through many problems during the years. We did a lot of hard work together and also had some nice times with our kids. While we lived on Bailey Ellsworth Road, Charlie and I were digging four maple trees to plant in our front yards when we heard a little dog barking at a big hollow tree. Charlie came up with a bright idea to have a little fun. He looked in the hollow and found a big old male groundhog, so he took off his old coat and said that I should use it to grab hold and hang on to the critter. He was then going to grab it by the tail and throw it to the ground.

Well, it was okay until old Chuck tore out through the back seam of the coat and ran over my shoulder and scratched the hell out of my neck. I turned and caught my heel on a tree root and fell on my left shoulder and popped it out of the socket and left it hanging in the front. I walked a mile home and will never forget that walk!

When our good friend and neighbor, Warren Trimbath, who held the mortgage on our little home, foreclosed on it, we were broke, all except for a horse, which I owed Stitles for or seven chickens; everything else that was salable, we had sold to pay the interest home, taxes, etc. So we put the house up for sale, but there were no buyers anywhere that had any money, and no bank or money lender would even talk about a loan, so we were, as they say, at the end of the rope. So Trimbath was about to start foreclosure when an old friend of school days stopped in to see us and said he and his wife of about three months were looking for a place to rent. They did not have enough money to buy a place, and they could not get financed on account of their age, and at that time, real estate was not very good collateral. So Jim and Blanche Brobst came back over the next morning and said if we could wait until they could check with their families to see if they could borrow $500. They also had a postal savings worth $600. So they said if that would let us salvage something after our loan was paid off, they would buy the place. Although it was hard thing to do, it was our only chance of not losing it all, so we ended up with $385. That was a bitter time for us and really started the beginning of the end for us.

Then I rented the former Stevens Level Factory. It was a cinder block construction and all one room except for a little room at either front corner with a large window in front of each and a big front entrance between that was an access to the main part of the building. We made a two-room apartment out of the one front room and added a kitchen to it. The other front corner we used for a gas station, plus a storage room and toilet. We used an old big metal tub for the bathtub. That left us a seventy-by-forty-foot floor space. I paid $35 per month for rent. Of course, we did not live in luxury, but the roof did not leak and the walls were solid. Well, I guess this was one of the worst years of my life. We just had less than $400, so I had to do the only thing that was available.

I heard that the Newton Steel was going to start operating again after being shut down for a long time. I talked to Ike Snyder, who had a gas station and also a bulk business on Canal Street. Ike was hurting, the same as all business people, along with everyone else. He told me if I would handle his supplies, he would help me stock a gas station. So in about a week, we got in the gas station business. My brother Burt helped for the first week or so. He had an Oakland car which was a great help to get us around until we got settled. We were just about a block from town at the corner of Milton Boulevard and Arlington Road across the street from the old wooden covered bridge.

I would like to forget about most of the next four years if possible, but of course, there were a few good things that happened that I will mention. Things went pretty good for one year until one Friday payday at the steel mill when the workers got notice with their checks that they were done and the mill was moving to Monroe, Michigan. That was like a stab in the heart to everybody in the area.

After that, there were a couple of things that happened that kept us from total collapse. Herb Biggard had the Chrysler and Plymouth agency but could not pay the rent on his rented building, so I let him have the back of our place for his agency and storage. Plus, I got the use of a car and sales rights. Well, let me tell you, there were not very many car buyers around in those days. I sold two cars in two years. I sold a used Chrysler coupe for $45 and a new 1935 Dodge to the owner of Bailey furniture store for $1,000, and the old guy insisted that I furnish a crank for it. So I had to send to the factory for one and it cost $4, which came out of my pocket. Herb had me help him get together a softball team to represent his Newton Auto Sales. Herb was a little overweight, but a real sport. He would have me bat flies to him in the vacant lot beside our building.

Herb had a lot of friends, and he was always a good friend to me. He tried to do many things to boost car sales, but there wasn't much that could help because money was so scarce. I did get a couple of little jobs installing frame parts in cars that had wooden doors and top frames that most cars had in those days. It was a kind of a tricky slow job because they were usually rotted and had to be formed by a rasp and drawshave. So I couldn't charge nearly what it was worth by the hour. But it sure did help pay the rent. A friend of Herb had a gas station in Warren on Pine Street with a partner. This partner had a heart problem and went to the Mayo Clinic in Boston. I took his half of the work over at the station. Alice and a neighbor ran our station while I worked three days a week in Warren. Of course, there were very few customers at our place. The only reason for staying was because there were no jobs anywhere. In the eight weeks I was at the station in Warren, we were robbed twice.

In 1937, I was in St. Joseph's Hospital to have my appendix removed. With me, I had an expensive gold watch that I acquired from trading a $15 car heater that was left over from the gas station closing. In those days, car heaters were not standard equipment on cars. A former mayor of Newton Falls had taken this Fifth Avenue Illinois watch as bail from a bootlegger, and he traded me even for the car heater. While I was in the hospital, I dropped it on the terrazzo floor and ruined it. Well, Clyde Jones knew of that watch deal and had asked me many times to trade it or sell it to him at a ridiculously low price, but I had traded with Clyde a couple of times, and he had cheated both times. So I waited several years to get even.

In the summer of 1937, Clyde stopped in one day to see Dad and to try to screw me out of that watch. He knew we were having money problems, so he made me several offers for the watch. I made up my mind to let him sweat but would not lie about it being broken beyond repair. I told him it had been running for a long time. I got it and let him look at it but told him that I was reluctant about selling it. He finally offered me $20 and an old watch for it. So I took the $20 and sent to a hatchery and got two hundred mixed-sex baby chicks at .10 cents each. A real deal even for those times. I guess the hatchery was really hurting as badly as we were. Well, we raised them and saved the hens for eggs and ate some of the roosters and sold the rest.

Then I went to the Republic Steel employment office and stood in line with many more poor guys begging for jobs. Well, out of a hundred or so, one or two might get taken in. Finally, after at least forty trips there, I got taken into the pickle acid house or "pickle house." The starting wage was .51 cents an hour or $4.80 a day, but after the first two weeks, we seldom worked a full week. They only ran the mill one order at a time, and most were small orders. Well, I was having nerve and stomach problems, not one good thing to look forward to. I guess that I just did not have brains enough to cope with the times. So our little family life ended in those crazy days.

In 1937, I married Frances Elizabeth Daugherty Marsh, who had a daughter named Phyllis Elaine. I had got acquainted with her after helping her when she had car problems along the road, and I stopped to help her.

Frances and Charles A. Jones   Frances and Phyllis   Phyllis and Ilene

We lived in a rented house on East Broad Street in Newton Falls for about one month. I was still working at the Republic Steel Mill, and Frances was working at Packard Electric. We then moved to Cora Saunders place on Salt Springs Road. It was just half mile west of where I was born. Archer Eugene was born September 13, 1938. We had quite a family the winter of 1938–39 in that little house. There were seven of us, my father, Arthur, my sister, Ilene, Phyllis, Betty, Bob, Archie, Fanny, and me. I was only getting a few days' work a week, and Dad only got a little repair job with very small pay. One time, he got eleven dozen eggs (which was one of his better jobs). In January and February of 1938, our pay came to $22 for two months. Well, we ate eggs, bread, potatoes, and creamed tomatoes for gravy on the potatoes. Well, we made it until spring. Dad got a job in Warren, and Ilene went to live with Mom, and the mill started to get a few orders for war steel, mostly from Japan and Russia, but not enough to work steady.

In 1938, I had Bill Kennedy plow a half-acre garden for me in exchange for farm labor for him, and also I got two quarts of milk every other day (we also used a lot of powdered milk). I sent to Salisbury, Maryland, and got four hundred strawberry plants at .10 cents each. They really did well; we sold some at the house, and Fanny took several crates to a store in Warren. She got .10 cents a quart for them. We had all the vegetables and sold a lot of parsnips and a few roasting chickens to fellows that I worked with at the mill.

In 1939, my uncle Dave and aunt Liz Kennedy lived across the road from us, and they were having trouble making payments on their fifty-five-acre farm. I asked them if they would be interested in selling a one acre lot off a corner of the farm to me to help with the mortgage on the place. They had a little three-room house beside their house that set up on blocks. It was awful cold living in it in the winter and hot in the summer, so it was bard to rent. They offered to sell it to me along with one and a half acres for $500 if I could pay their mortgage payments until they could get it paid up or until my $500, plus interest, was paid. Well, we scraped the bottom for a year or so, but then we finally owned our first home.

In 1940, Dad told me that a friend of his was going to build a house, and he thought that I could get the job. I didn't waste any time going to see about that! I got the first contract I ever had to build a house. That was a real big day for Fanny and me. Just getting into business was a lot of work and headaches, but it was the start of a better feeling in life. I finally had a job that I could go to and make enough money to support my family. We never had a lot of money, but it always was enough to eat and live an almost normal life.

Well, I built several more houses, plus many repair jobs, before the war effort got us little guys. Then rationing laws took us out. We couldn't even buy a nail or anything that was not rationed, except most foods and clothing, and even some of them were not available without ration stamps.

Jack Hugh was born there in 1941, and in the spring, Fanny got a problem with Aunt Liz. She was very bossy and tried to run our lives. I decided to move our house to the other side of our lot, which was three hundred feet, farther away from their house, and give us a little more privacy. Even so, we managed to stay good friends with them.

I found a man who had three twenty-four-feet eight-by-eight oak timbers to sell for $30. I already had several two-by-ten planks, so I went to the Wayland Basket factory and bought twelve four-by-forty-two-inch rolls. They were the centers left from lathe timbers (they cost .10 cents each). Charlie Sheldon and George Davis both had worked for a building mover at one time, and they were out of work, so they offered to help me for $4 a day. With their help, we rolled that little house on the timbers and planks with the rollers between. Even with the ground being soft and a six-foot-wide ditch to cross, we managed to move it with the help of my little gallant western horse and a pulley block in just three long days.

We dug our own well at that place as soon as we could after moving, but we had to haul our water in ten gallon milk cans until we got it dug. We bought six two-foot tile. We would sink one tile, then I would get inside the tile and fill buckets with dirt and Fanny would pull them up with a rope. We got good water at twelve-foot depth. I then dug a cellar under the house. It was a slow hard job! Fanny was pregnant with Fanny Dale, but she was really a brave woman and devoted mother and wife. I could never have made it without her!

I built another room on the house with the help of my horse Nancy. I used a slip scraper to dig a basement so we had a little more space.

Our place was bordered on the east by my uncle Bid Kennedy's farm. He had a pulsating electric fence around a field along the side of our drive. Archer was about four years old and was playing by skipping alongside of the fence, patting the wire as he skipped along. He was warned by his mom, and I never to cross the drive, but he was just being adventurous as boys often are. Fortunately, he must have managed to touch the wire between pulses and didn't get shocked but did get spanked.

We had an outside toilet, and it had a screen-door hinge on it to keep it closed. It would slam shut if not eased shut. One day, I was in a hurry when leaving and let the dang thing slam and was just taking my first step out when I thought someone hit my back with a ball bat or club. But I discovered that a hornet had been annoyed by the bang and got angry and stung me on the back between my shoulders.

One cold winter, we had a strange houseguest. We were just relaxing reading one evening, and I heard a strange noise outside. I thought at first that it might be the wind blowing some object against the house, so I went out and looked around and saw a possum walking around the house wall on his hind legs, reaching up and clawing at the cellar window, trying to get in. Well, it was awful cold out, so I got a box and put him in it and gave him a little piece of bologna. He devoured it like the hungry critter he was, so I found a few more things for him to eat and secured a lid on the box and kept it in the cellar that night so the kids could see it the next morning. Well, as you might guess, that critter was our guest and well-fed by the kids until the next spring. When we said goodbye to our little friend, the kids were so unhappy we got them two kittens to take its place.

That following summer, we fixed a box in the backyard and fed and kept them outside, except when the kids brought them in to play with them. We had a pie pan beside their box for their feed. I went out one day and saw Archer and Jack down on their hands and knees eating the kittens' bread and milk. So then we felt we had four kittens, but the law said the two newest ones had to sleep and be fed inside.

I had an old sow pig that was pregnant. The night before or the day she gave birth to seven little ones, she disappeared. We looked for her for four days. On the fifth evening, I went across the road and found where she had been rooting around for roots and acorns. I saw where a big tree had been uprooted. She had made a nest under the uprooting, and her little ones were cuddled up in the nest. When I went near, she came at me with her mouth wide-open, so I went back and got a bucket of feed for her, but she wouldn't follow me for the feed.

While I was trying to figure some way to get her back home, my friend Charlie Sheldon came over to visit. He came up with an idea that sounded good to me. He suggested that we take several ears of corn and put it away from the nest so we could lure her out and catch one of the little ones. Well, just as Charlie and I started out with the corn, my brother Floyd and his father-in-law, Ben Wagner, drove in to see me about a job getting a house ready for them to plaster. They decided to help us get the pigs rounded up. We waited awhile for the sow to get far enough away so we could get to one of the little ones. Charlie got one first, and it started to squeal; that old sow came back mad as hell, and Charlie took off for the sow house with the baby pig in his arms. The sow followed him as far as the road fence, then whirled around and came back after us. She was coming at me with her mouth wide-open.

I tried to scare her off, but she was not stopping. I jumped out of her way and started climbing a little tree, and before I was off the ground, Ben put his hand on my head and went up that tree right over top of me. I don't know if the pig was afraid or if she was amused by the comedy, but she just turned and went back after Charlie and her squalling baby. Charlie got the little guy in the pen, and she followed it in. We brought the rest of her little pigs back to her, and all were happy. Then we all had a glass of cider.

I never paid much attention to politics before, but since I had just recently become a landowner, I figured that made me a more respectable citizen. So one day, I was listening to a group of farmers discussing politics. I asked one of the fellows who was one of the better dressed ones, "How do guys as ignorant as I am know who to vote for?" He said the best way for me to vote would be for me to see how my boss voted, then vote just the opposite. Well, that man was a Republican and, I believe, the only one I have ever seen who wasn't so biased that if he started in one direction, he would meet himself coming back. I believe he was one of a very few of his kind. And in this year of 2001, it hasn't changed very much.

Frances used to babysit for a lady on Route 45, and she always told me how she would like to have that house if it was ever up for sale and we could afford to buy it. Well, we finally got the chance a couple of years later. Althea Lutz was the administrator for her parents' estate. She had two brothers who would sign off, so she sent them word that she wanted to sell and move to Warren where she worked at Packard Electric. We were waiting to hear the asking price when, one day, she called Frances and told her if she could come up with $2,500 cash real soon, we could have the place. I thought I was dreaming when I heard that. I told Fanny to call her back and make sure that was the right price. She said it was right if we could get the cash right away, so I put myself in gear and headed for the First Federal Bank to see about a loan. George Watson was president then, so I went right up to him and asked him about getting a loan. After looking at a map of the place, he called his secretary of the bank, Al Goss, and talked to him about it, and they agreed that it was a good deal, and I got the loan.

We called a real estate man, Roy Westover, whom I had known for a long time and asked him if he could sell our place. He had a very successful business in Warren and, after ending the winter in Florida, was happy to start getting his business in Warren going again. He called about three days later and said he thought he had a buyer. We sold the house for $2,200.

Around that time, we got a little Jersey cow that played a big part in helping raise our family. We had her with us for fourteen years. I had trouble with my car on my home from work one day about three miles from home. A farmer saw me as I was walking down the road and asked if he could help me, and I told him I had a part at home to fix it. Just about then, his son Jim came from inside the barn and asked his dad what he should do with a little runt of a calf that had just been born that morning. He told Jim to hit it in the head and bury it. I spoke up and said that if they were going to do that I would like to have it. That made Jim and I both happy! I walked home with the little critter's belly over the back of my neck and my arms around its legs. I'm sure Fanny must have wondered what or where my mind was. Well, I have wondered about that same thing many times myself.

Anyway, that Suzy turned out to be a very important addition to our family. She kept us supplied with milk and butter for twelve years. And with Fanny's great art with the sewing machine, the printed muslin bags that the cow feed came in provided shirts and dresses and playclothes for the family. I really think she deserves all the time I have spent to tell this story. I mean, both Fanny and Suzy.

Suzy, source of milk and butter

Back of the house after much work

Well, I guess I had better mention the condition of that old seven-room house. It was built in the middle 1800s and had not had very good care for a long time. Of course, no inside plumbing and the old outside toilet was about to fall apart. The inside of the house was filthy! It had cat shit in the corner of the dining room, a hole the size of a football in the kitchen that had been covered over by an old piece of cardboard under the worn-out linoleum that I stepped through the first day we lived there. There was an outside cellar way with a cover or door.

There were two goat stalls just inside the opening that were a foot deep with straw and goat shit. We cleaned all that out and put it on the garden. I nailed a board over the hole in the kitchen, and we dug the cat shit out of the corners with putty knives and a rag over our noses. The outside wasn't any better: the old lap siding was bare of paint and badly weathered, the back side was worse, there were a couple of places that had split boards and several holes, all the windows needed puttied, and the roof leaked.

Well, I suppose by reading the above you wonder why a carpenter, or anyone, would buy such a dump. There were several reasons: Frances wanted to live there. There were 30 acres of prime land on a main road with 650 feet frontage on Route 45 and 3,000 feet on Tait Road. It was flat iron shape with about 300 feet across the back.

There was one drawback not mentioned before. There was a little old garage at the north side of the driveway that had no doors and was ready to collapse and the wood was mostly bad. Bud Ready, who was manager at North Jackson Lumber, had one of his men load it on one of their trucks and haul it away, no charge.

There was no barn on the property, so we kept Suzy in a corner of that old garage until we got a two-story building from Lee and Marguerite Daugherty who had bought the farm south of us right after we moved to our place. We were able to move it to our place with the help of a set of rented moving equipment and two of Jim Brobst's tractors. Of course, Jim came with them for a very small fee. I put a box stall in for the cow and used the rest of it for storage and a haymow above. I put a sliding door for a tractor entrance in the front and a hinged door in back for the cow.

I bought red paint for the sides and white for the trim and set them in the barn until I had time to paint. A couple of days later, I thought I would start to paint, but the paint was gone! I looked everyplace I could think of but couldn't find it, so I asked Fanny and the kids if they had seen it, but no one seemed to know anything about it. I was beginning to think I had lost a few, or perhaps a lot, of my marbles. But a day or two later, I happened to look back toward the pasture and saw a little hut that was painted pink, so I think you can guess where my red and white paint went. Strange things do happen when you raise a family!

Kay Ellen was born June 3, 1944, which was a real busy time for all of us, but we were all happy with a little girl. Now we had three girls, and with my Betty Jean, and they all turned out to be four great girls! We had a home large enough for all of us, and Fanny was as happy as I was. We seemed to have a better future ahead of us. Fanny had the home she loved!

When we lost the pine trees to a storm

Now before I get ahead of time, I think that I should say a few things about my time on the volunteer fire department and also the government fire department.

As you know, it takes an interested person to get any organization going and then a pusher to keep it going. Well, I was not a pusher or an organizer, but I was interested, so with the help of Barry Doyle, a good guy who was assistant chief of the depot department and another old friend Ed Kibler, plus goodwill from the community and the Lordstown trustees we got started. Of course, there were many more people that I haven't named who were also a big help. As in all organizations, there is always a few that get more time in than others, but that is just part of this life. Anyway, we were fortunate to have a good bunch of guys that were charter members. We started out by electing officers, then we appointed groups for different projects. First, we went to work on the old two-story building that had a family living on the second floor. We made an agreement with Mrs. Messersmith the occupant to tend the telephone and operate the alarm system in exchange for their rent, electric, water, and sewer. She did a good job for many years.

The fire department put on plays and had ice-cream socials and turkey suppers to raise money to help buy boots, hats, coats, etc., because, at that time, the township had very little tax money coming in, and it took most of it for road work. But we had good trustees and a clerk who was very good at understanding our needs.

I was able to get Cloyd Grimm, the clerk, and Tom Lohr, a trustee to join the department. One of the first things we did was concrete the lower floor. The trustees ordered us a new fire truck from a firm in Columbus, Ohio. Then came the plumbing, electric, and other things that needed done to the old building. We later added a kitchen and a meeting room.

Front row: Whitey Montgomery, Bernie Waechter,
Captain Bus Mat hews, Asst. Chief Paul Elsesscr, Chief
Arch Jones, Ed Kibler, Cloyd Grimm, Bob Kreitler
Back row: Tom Taylor, Floyd Jones, Burt Jones, Al Romain,
Eugene Montgomery, Jimmy Messersmith Bob Martin, Bob
Huffman, Elmer Harner, Norman Montgomery, Clarence Cole,
Elmer Nedrow Tom Lohr, Bob Tillett, Jay Kistler, Bob Platt

Before the new truck arrived, we decided to build a tanker truck ourselves. Bus Mathews, who was a real go-getter took task over and did a good job of it. It was an international truck with a five-hundred-gallon pump and a ten-thousand-gallon tank. We converted an old Packard ambulance into an emergency car and bought some equipment for it. We all put in a lot of time and work, but all seemed to be happy doing it.

One time, I had a friend of mine speak at a meeting. I had played ball against a guy named Bill McKinley who later became an American League umpire. He talked about his experiences as an umpire. He talked a lot about Luke Easter, mostly about his size, and how he was so big he got in his own way. Things were different then. Bill's salary as a major league umpire was $4,600 a year. He worked in his brother's butcher shop in Kinsman during the winter months to help pay his bills.

Frances was a big help to me by helping to organize a ladies auxiliary for the volunteer department. Thanks to them and a helpful community, all of plays, turkey suppers, and ice-cream socials were all successful for many years.

This will concern my time working at the Lordstown Ordinance Depot from 1943 to 1948. I started as first-class fireman. There were two stations on the base. Number 1 station was in the front of the property and number 2 was in the back. Number 1 had eighteen beds and a space in the corner for the assistant chief's desk. In the other corner, there were two card tables—the chief's and secretary's office. There was a big bathroom and shower on one side of a hallway and a kitchen and furnace room on the other and a hall and four steps to the truck room, and systems and workroom.

We worked twenty-four hours on and twenty-four off. We had nine warehouses and six open sheds, each nine thousand feet long, to inspect for fire safety every evening after the workforce was done. We took turns, each man inspecting three buildings once a week. We also had to make our beds Army style, do all the house cleaning, including windows, and take care of the trucks and all the other fire equipment. I ate breakfast at home and worked carpenter work on my days off. I ate two meals at the depot when working there.

One day, we were out testing a pump on a pond, and one of the firemen that was holding the hose decided to take his false teeth out and hold them in front of the nozzle to wash them off. Well, the water pressure was at about 150 pounds, so his teeth flew about 125 feet into the pond. The water was only about 2 1/2 feet deep in that area of the pond, so he waded around in that pond for an hour and darned if he didn't find them.

The first six months I was there, I spent a lot of my time just getting acquainted with a different way of life. I was not used to having so much idle time on my hands, and I was soon bored and hunting things to do. I told Doyle about it, and he started to find little projects around the station for me to do. I built a coat and boot rack, made a storage cabinet, and installed shelves in the bedroom, kitchen, and chief's office. I also helped Pete Corall in the kitchen, even made wooden toys for kids' Christmas. I was advanced three times in rank and pay while there—from fireman to truck driver to crew chief. We were also assigned to medic duty on Sunday at the hospital and was instructed by the nurse and doctor to give only aspirin to anyone who came with any ailment from a headache to broken leg. The dose was from one to six, depending on the seriousness of the ailment.

One time, I was scalded on the feet from hot water in my boots, and I told the nurse that I was allergic to aspirin, so she gave me two shots of whiskey and I survived.

We had a few in the group on my turn that preferred to eat supper separate from rest of us. Those of us that did eat together put money in a pot, and one of the members would bring the food ordered by Pete Corall, who was the cook most of the time.

John DiAngelis was an Italian fellow that made the best spaghetti that I ever tasted. We were able to get him to cook for us about three times a month. He would always ask me to bring a quart of tomatoes that Fanny canned with one hot pepper in it. We would do his inspection and other daily chores while he spent the whole day cooking. He was a former Youngstown bootlegger, but he was a good guy.

We had people in that fire department from all different walks of life, and most were good guys. We had schoolteachers, farmers, bookkeepers, shoe salesmen, bus drivers, clerks, carpenters, concrete finishers, masons, factory workers, and a magician—men from every walk of life.

I kind of think they were lucky we had only a few fires that really took a lot of exertion because there was just a few of those men that were in shape to do hard work. We did have many small fires, some we put out with just hand extinguishers, but we did have one big fire that was in one of the open sheds where the shipping boxes and crates were built. There were piles of lumber and a shop for the tools and an enclosed office that took up about one-fourth of the shed. The rest was filled with other combustible materials. The flames went 100 feet in the air, and it was so hot we had to keep water on a warehouse that was 130 feet from it to keep it from catching on fire. The tire had started in a scrap box that contained wood scraps, shavings, etc., so it got a real big start before the fire department was called. I had just gotten home and was eating my breakfast when our phone rang, and I had to go back on duty for twenty-four more hours. That was when I got my feet scalded. There were seven fire trucks and twenty-four men busy for twenty-four hours. We saved about half of the contents, but the structural part was lost. The building was 960 feet long, 80 feet wide, and 20 feet high made from all red fir timbers.

One day, I was out checking one of the trucks around back of the depot property next to the south fence, and a beautiful big buck deer ran in front of me and along the fence. He stopped for about a minute while I sat and watched him. He decided to get away from that big red fire truck and me, so he just jumped over the eight-foot fence so gracefully I couldn't believe it.

The guards had six horses they rode to patrol the fence line. They were kept in a big barn near the main gate in back of the commanding officer's house. There were fire extinguishers on both floors of the barn that had to be checked every day. That was one of the jobs that some of the fellows tried to avoid because there were a lot of rats running all through the barn, and the nut that was in charge of the barn had a superstition that rats would warn of any trouble around. So he wouldn't let anyone try to get rid of them.

Things seemed to be on a civil level while the war was on, but so many things took place after that I was not very happy to work there anymore. I never did understand why, but the government put Sears Roebuck and their people in to manage the depot for one year in place of the Army. Well, it was during that time of the Sears management that we had that big fire, and I actually heard one of the Sears big shots say, "Well, that was a good way to take some of that stuff off the market," meaning, the stuff that had burned. I never felt right working there after that.

And I did quit for one year, the spring of 1947, and started back to full-time carpenter work. I built three houses that year with a couple of little repair jobs. One house was for my brother Floyd and his wife, Clara, on a lot we sold them from the northwest corner of the farm. Work started to get slack again in 1948. John Gessner stopped in to see me one day and asked me if I would come back to the depot at top fireman's pay. So I went back, but after a year, I could see that the depot was closing out, and working two jobs was getting to be too much. I was feeling tired all the time. So I went back to contracting and stayed at carpentry until I retired. I had more jobs coming than I could take care of, so I had to have more help. I took my brother Burt in with me and then Ed Kibler. We did very well together. We did general construction, which was very satisfying work. It never got boring; there was always a lot of different people to deal with and associate with—some good and some a bit... But most were real good. And always, things to keep my mind is to look forward and not back at the past.

Charles and Burt at work

That was an era of many good times, but some sad and hectic times. One of the sad times was in 1945 when Dad died of heart failure in Tolison, Arizona. We had been writing back and forth quite often, and he was planning on returning back to Ohio. Frances and I were going to give him a lot off our farm to build a cottage on, but to our sorrow, he died just a few days before he intended to leave Arizona. He was buried in Pine View Cemetery in Warren.

Arthur Jones in Arizona

One of the good things that happened was that we had a baby boy, James Arthur Jones, born on April 16, 1946. One of the hectic times was when he was about one year old; he got the measles and then got whooping cough along with it. He was very ill, but we could not get him into a hospital because of the measles. We called a doctor and waited, and when he didn't show up, we called another doctor. He came right away and said we would have to get Jim on oxygen right away as he was having a hard time breathing. He was panting like a dog does when out of breath. Well, that was in war times, and the government had everything tied up so tight that all oxygen units were not available.

Since I worked at the depot, across the road, I asked the nurse at the hospital there if we could borrow a tank from her, but she said it was against government regulations to let it out of government property. Well, I happened to think of Harry Doyle being pretty well up on fire department procedures, and he told me that I should call the Warren City Fire Department and ask if they would help me even though we were six miles from the city limits. So I called and told them the situation, and the person who answered said he would ask Chief Oldacres if they could help me. Well, thank God, when he heard of our plight, he said to hell with regulations; he would send help right away.

Within ten minutes, three firemen drove in with a oxygen tank and also a new piece of equipment donated to the department by the Moose Lodge of Warren. They had never used the portable lung before, so between the doctor and the firemen, they had to decide whether to use the iron lung or the oxygen. They decided on the iron lung, which turned out to be a really good choice as fifteen minutes after the mask was in place, Jim started to breathe regularly. There were two men who came out twice a day for three days, then once a day for four days after. Finally, the doctor said Jim was well enough to breathe on his own.

When Jim was just a bit over two years old, Fanny went to town one day, taking the little girls and Jim. Jim didn't want to let anyone take his hand but would walk along beside them. Well, there were a lot of people on the sidewalk those days as parking places were scarce. Fanny stopped to look in a store window, and she turned around and Jim was gone. The girls and her couldn't find him, so she went three blocks to the police station to see if they had heard of or seen Jim. They told her there was a little boy at the fire station next door. She went there and found Jim sitting on a fireman's shoulder, being shown a fire truck. It turned out that the fireman that was entertaining him was one of the firemen that came out with the iron lung when he was so sick.

I'll back track a couple of years to when I first started to work for myself. I bought an old two-wheeled trailer for $15 to haul my tools, lumber, etc., with. Well, it was okay but awfully unhandy to haul long lumber and was dangerous on the road. One day, when I was going down the road with a load of scaffolding planks, I hit a low place with one wheel. That trailer started to shimmy like a gandy dancer and almost wrecked the car and threw planks all in the path of another car coming from the other way, but he got stopped just in time or it might have wrecked him also. Well, I picked up my tools and planks and went home. We had a couple of dollars in a dresser drawer, so I went uptown and paid a third down on a $150 Chevy panel truck at Pritchard Auto Sales. That was a lot better because I could keep my tools out of the weather. I used that truck until 1950 when I bought a 1949 Dodge pickup truck with heavy duty frame, wheels, etc.

We had a pretty good life while living on that little farm on Route 45. Of course, we also had a few scars along the way.

In 1948, I was working two jobs, and we were doing okay, and I had a couple bucks saved, so I bought a cub tractor and some equipment to do a little farming on fourteen of our acres and a half acre for vegetables. Before that, I had one horse and my brother-inlaw Lee Daugherty had one horse, so to save money, we traded and took turns using them. The horse I had was a pretty sorrel named Belle. I bought her from Bill Kennedy when we were changing from horses to tractors. They had six horses and wanted to cut the extra work and feeding and caring for them. Belle was the youngest of the six and had never been broken or even had a harness on. Bill sold her to me for $35 with rope and halter. As I led her home, I passed by the Cassidy farm, and Harry was out at his mailbox. Well, we talked a little about the weather, and he asked me what I was going to do with a young unbroken horse. I told him that I was going to plow my garden the next day. He smiled and wished me luck, thinking I had lost my marbles.

Well, I took her home and combed her good and got her used to my talking and petting her and just letting her know that I was going to be kind to her. The next day, I put the harness on her and let her get used to this strange thing she had never experienced before. Then I hitched her up with the other horse and plowed my garden. She and Belle worked together real good. Proving that attention with kindness pays.

One of our activities while we were there was fighting rats. They used to keep horses in a barn across the street at the depot. When the government started to shut down operations, they got rid of the horses. Of course, the barn was cleaned of grains, so the rats left there and came across the road to our place. Well, in about a week after they took horses away, we were overrun with the dirty rats. They got in the house, the garage, the barn, pigpen, strawstack, and everywhere. They would even run over our feet while we were milking the cows. We bought poison, but they seemed to be immune to it.

About that time, we had an *experience* with the boys. I got the boys a BB gun for Christmas. Well, they experimented with them and tried shooting all kinds of things in them besides BBs. They found that wooden matches would fit in the end of the barrel, and when shot at something rough like a rock, they would light. Well, one day, coming home for lunch, I saw a cloud of smoke when I was about a mile away from home, and it looked like it might be close to our place, so I hurried home. I found a fire truck in my drive along with several firemen. They had wet the barn down to keep it from burning, but the strawstack was gone. The boys said they were in the house eating their lunch when the fire had started. Well, I was not a witness and no one else had seen it start, so I let it pass, but I had an idea of my own about how it got started.

When that strawstack burned, the firemen said that a lot of rats ran out of it, but I suppose that most of them stayed with us. One night, I went downstairs to get a drink of water or else pee. Anyhow, when I got down there, I saw two big rats up on the back of the couch. I made up my mind right then to start a war on rats. I never did like rats, but I now hate them. The next night, it got worse. I was awakened in the middle of the night by a noise on the stairs, so I got up and saw a big rat at the top of the steps. It ran into the boy's bedroom. Fanny heard me cussing the rat and came out to help me chase it. We each grabbed a shoe of hers and went after it. It went over the top of the boys while they were lying in bed and all around and through the four bedrooms and two closets. We would whack it with the heel of a shoe every time we could get it cornered until, finally, after about half an hour, it stopped. I beat that rat until it was like a dishrag. Fanny finally said, "That's enough Arch."

I finally thought of an idea to get rid of them. If people committed suicide by hooking a hose to a car exhaust, then why not kill rats the same way? The next day was Sunday with all the kids home to help. My brother Floyd had a little dog that enjoyed killing rats, so I called him, and he said he was happy to bring little Penny to help. I got an old vacuum hose and attached it to the exhaust pipe of the cub tractor and into a hole under the barn floor and started the tractor. In about thirty seconds, the rats started to come out of there.

She grabbed them as fast as she could, and Floyd and I clubbed the rest as they came out. We did that same thing at every hole we could find in the other buildings also. We killed twenty-three rats that day, and with the help of a couple of good cats, we were never bothered by rats at that place again as long as we lived there.

In the winter of 1949 and 1950, we had the biggest snowstorm that I can remember in our area. There were many people snowed in for several days. The snow was anywhere from twenty-four to thirty-six inches deep and drifted up to eighteen feet. At the depot furnace rooms, the snow was drifted clear to the roof on the sides and the janitors had a full-time job just keeping a path to the doors. They took a D-9 bulldozer to plow the snow away from the back because the truck snowplow could not do the job. Even then the bulldozer buried itself up to the driver on the seat.

I put chains on my tractor and was able to get my drive open out to the road, which they kept plowing all day because of the government depot. I plowed Floyd's drive so he could get out and he had a set of chains, so we took his truck and went to Warren and got a set of chains for my truck. We found five more sets and took them home for neighbors for their vehicles so they could get to work.

The neighbor that lived across the road from me before the government took over the farm still owned a fifty-acre pasture next to our place. He lived in Warren but kept about twenty head of beef cattle there. There was a shed for the cattle to get in out of the bad weather, but the night of the big snow, the shed doors blew shut. The next morning, I found them standing all in a group outside the shed in snow up above their bellies and a coat of snow on their backs. The snow was so deep they couldn't move, so I put two bales of hay on the tractor and went over and broke a path to the shed and got the door open. Then I had a hard time getting those cows to go in. I guess they were so cold it was hard for them to move.

Fanny and Pet Raccoon

Kay and Same Raccoon

Jim, Jack, Archer, Fanny

Jack, Kay, Jim, Fanny, Archer

Jim and Mutt

Archer, Fanny Dale, Jim, Kay, Jack

I wasn't a very good scholar, and quitting school did not make me a very bright person, so of course, I have done some awful stupid things. But I still had dreams, and two of them were to see the state of Oregon and to see Australia. Jim was just seven and Archer was fifteen when Fanny and I decided we should all go to Oregon. So one day in April 1953, Fanny went scouting for a mobile unit that would accommodate all seven of us. She found a mobile home that would do for us to travel with. In May, after selling everything we owned, except the farm (we rented it to an officer from the depot), we took off with the old 1946 Dodge truck and a 1948 Plymouth car and five kids and drove 2,865 miles to Eugene Oregon.

Our home away from home

Well, it was quite a trip! I had five tires blow out on the truck and one on the automobile. Of course, we were overloaded in all the vehicles. I had thought that we were safe on the tire problem when we started out as I had bought four for the car and two for the truck and two for the mobile home. But due to some rough roads and being overloaded, we had problems. Fanny got awful bored driving so slow and got tired from the long hours on the road. My top speed was 45 mph and down to 5 mph going up and over the mountains. We took the old Oregon Trail. I had a problem with air lock in the fuel system and boiling radiator also. We had to carry cans of water to wet rags to lay over the gas line and fill the radiator. One time, we ran out of water and I had to get a half grapefruit from the mobile home and slit it. Then I straddled it over the gas line; it did the job! The natives in the mountains carried canvas bags about one foot square hung by a strap over their radiator caps to get moisture to their motors. Gas prices ranged from .22 cents a gallon to a high of .43 cents but averaged at .28 cents a gallon.

I had a bit of a problem going up the east side of the Sheridan Pass in Wyoming. It was twenty-six miles to the top, and I had to use low gear all the way and was very concerned about making it to the top when a truck driver came along side of me and said he was worried about me also. So he drove behind me from about halfway up to the top. He said he could block me from going backward if my truck should stall. He had a big Kenworth cattle truck, and I was pulling that mobile home with a little three-speed Dodge pickup. We were on the road for nine and a half days and got awful tired. But the kids got to see and experience things they all say they enjoyed and they remember it as a good time in their life. So perhaps one of my blunders was not a total bad one after all.

On the way to Oregon, we met Fanny's sister, Carolyn, her daughter, Sharon, and her husband, Lawrence Kitchen, between Burns and Bend, Oregon. They were on a vacation from their home in Rosemead, California, and decided to meet us and surprise us. Well, needless to say, we were happy to see someone we knew as we had been on the road for seven days and hadn't seen anyone we knew since leaving Lordstown. We stopped and ate lunch together near a little town called Riley. We then drove on for a few miles to about five miles east of Brothers and pulled off to the side of the road. We stopped early for the night because we were all tired. There wasn't enough room for all nine of us in the mobile, so Lawrence and I slept outside on Army cots they had with them.

Jack, Archer, Charles, Frances, Fanny Dale,
Jim, and Kay on the way to Oregon

We had a thrill on the last lap of our trip just before we got to Eugene. We were going down the Willamette Pass. Fanny was in the front car, the Kitchens were next, and Archer and Jack were with me in the truck. Well, they were getting restless after riding nine days in the hot cab of the truck, and they started to elbow one another in the ribs. During the tussle, they hit the gear shift lever and knocked it out of gear, and we had just started down. I tried to slow down with the brakes, but they got hot and didn't hold; the motor revved up and sounded like a jet. I was looking for the engine to fly up through the hood, but I finally jammed it into second gear, and that was when that old motor did roar. I did happen to have brains enough to blow the horn and alert Lawrence to get out of my way, and he waved at Fanny to speed up. Finally, all was clear, but I was sure all of us had one of the fastest rides we had ever had. When we pulled into a gas station a little while later, I couldn't hold a bottle of pop still enough to drink it.

We pulled into Eugene on a Sunday about noon and started looking for a trailer park. We passed one that was nice and classy looking, and we thought it would be too expensive for us, so we went on a few miles farther and stopped at a little old-looking park but only took it for one day. We wanted to look around a get a bit more acquainted with the area. So the next day, we went back, and while passing the Shamrock Mobile Park, we saw an old man sitting on a chair, waving his hand at us to stop and come in. I stopped, and he said he had seen us drive past yesterday and figured we were looking for a place to park our mobile home. He said he bet that we thought his place would be too high priced, but it was wasn't. He said that he would give us a special price since we had a big family.

He cut off $5 a month and charged us $20 a month, water and sewage furnished, and there was a real nice laundry and the Willamette River was just one thousand feet from our lot. The river was very shallow but real wide in that area, so the kids could wade in it without danger of drowning. We had a young couple that lived beside us that always went with them to play in the water. The water in most streams in Oregon those days was pure enough to drink, and we did. Our water supply to the mobile was piped underground and then a pipe about a foot high to our hose to the inside, and the manager of park said that he only had the pipes freeze in the winter twice in two years. Another good thing about that valley was that we never saw lightning in the valley. But up in the surrounding mountains, it flashed like Fourth of July fireworks.

The Kitchens stayed and helped us get situated and then took off for home Tuesday morning. On Wednesday morning, I went to the carpenters' union office to see about a job and get a transfer to their order. While I was getting that fixed up, a young man came in and said he needed a finish carpenter. So the business agent asked me if I was available and could do finish work, and I said yes to both of his questions. He introduced me to the young Charles Courtney, and he told me I could start on a finish job for him the next day at eight in the morning at a new office for a feed mill.

It was close to downtown Eugene, and I parked on the street in the front door and just got in the front door when an older man came over and shook hands and asked my name. He said his name was Sig Tutthen; he took a pack of Cavalier cigarettes out of his pocket and asked me to have one. Well, I did smoke at that time, but I never liked those damned Cavaliers. But I took one since he was such a friendly man. I was sorry after that even though I was a smoker as he never let up on shaking a pack of them damned Cavaliers at me and seemed disappointed when I refused them. I finally said to him, "Sig, you must buy a lot of cigarettes," and he said, "I do, but it makes my wife happy because she gets such nice things with all the coupons." He was a real nice buddy anyway.

About noon that day, a policeman came in and asked whose green Plymouth that was out in front, and I thought, *What the hell is wrong with parking it there?* I asked him what the problem was, and he told me that I hadn't put any sign on it to indicate it was a worker's car. I asked him what I must do to get a tag for that, and he said he knew that I was new there and probably didn't know their laws so he would tag it for me. So he went out and picked up a little piece of wood and laid it on the hood of the car and said, "Now it's legal." And believe it or not, that was all it took to be law-abiding.

From our first day, there we never met anyone in Oregon who was not friendly. They made us feel like we were old friends from day one until we left. Well, not quite true. When we moved to Reedsport, it was time for my driver's license renewal. I went to get it renewed, and the guy in charge gave me a book of rules to take home and study overnight. I took him that I thought I could pass their test right then as I had been driving for over twenty years and thought I knew most of the driving laws. I didn't want to miss another day's work if I could take the test while I was already there. Well, he had an ugly look on his face and said to go out in my car and study the book for a while. Well, I went out and looked at that damned book for about half an hour and went back in and told him I was ready to take the test, and he slammed a paper on the desk and said if I didn't pass the test that I would have to wait thirty days before I could take it again.

Well, I was pissed off by the way he acted, so I said I would take it anyhow, and that didn't improve our relationship at all. When I got the form filled out, I gave it to him, and after looking at it for a while, he stuck it under the counter and said I had passed, but he thought that I might have cheated a little, but he gave me my license.

The kids adapted to their new home right away, and the young folks that lived next to us were like teenagers and played with our kids and looked after them like they were part of the family. Their last name was Dalton and claimed to be descendants of the famed old Dalton gang. The young man said his uncle was a son of one of the old gang and was in Western movies in Hollywood.

I worked a week or so on the feed mill and got acquainted with the crew that worked for Courtney and a lot of other people who just stopped in to see what was going on because there wasn't very much construction in progress in that area at that time.

One morning, Courtney came to me and took me to a corner away from the other guys and asked me if I would like a little raise in wages. He said he needed a capable person to look after the remodeling of a store building as he would be out of town for a while. Well, since I was the newest man he had working for him and one of them was the chairman of the carpenter union and another was the secretary, I felt like I was in a bind. I told him that I'd rather give the job to one of the older workers since I was the newest man. He said he wanted me, and if anything was said, they could talk to him since he was informing them about it right then. Well, I decided that I would try it and that if it worked out okay I would stay. Well, only one man did anything about it, and that was my old Swedish friend Sig. He didn't say a word about it, but he cut down on the number of times a day that he offered me those damned Cavalier cigarettes, which was okay by me, but we did remain friends.

Courtney must have thought that Sig had a little bad feelings about it, so he sent him to a job at Oakridge doing farmwork on a schoolhouse, and I went to work at the shoe store job in town. The next job was in Goshen, about ten miles west of Eugene, to remodel a grocery store. It had a wooden floor, and the lumberjacks, who were the majority of customers in that area, all wore spikes on their shoes, and they cut the floor so badly that it was almost through in places. The owner decided that a concrete floor would discourage them from wearing their spikes in the store.

When that job was done, Courtney asked me if I would like to move to another place that was away from Eugene where he had a job that would last a year and that it would be a great place for the family near the ocean. I told him we all were satisfied where we were. He said he didn't have enough work to keep me busy for the winter as he had contracted to build twenty-three houses for a big plywood company in Reedsport. He said he needed me there and if I was willing he would find me a place to put our mobile home. So I talked to Fanny and the kids about it, and we decided to move even though we would miss the Willamette Valley.

The next week, Courtney stopped in where I was working and said he had a nice place rented for us to park for $15 a month. The water, sewage, and garbage were furnished, and we were just across the street from the housing project where I would be working. It was near the mouth of the Umpqua River about a quarter of a mile from the town of Reedsport, so it was a real handy place for us to live.

We left Eugene on a Sunday morning and went south to the pear country, then west and followed the Umpqua River through the beautiful Douglas fir forests and the West Coast mountain range to the Pacific Ocean, and then we arrived in Reedsport about 4:00 p.m.

Reedsport was a small town on the south side of the mouth of the Umpqua River, and we lived about one-half mile from downtown on the back of the last lot on the street. It was as Charlie said, just across from the project. I just had to walk across the road to my job, so Fanny had the car right at home whenever she wanted it. The kids had an unlimited area of fir forest and a mountain to explore. On the weekends, we went for rides on the back roads where we could see the beauty of nature as the Lord left it in the unspoiled stage before us damned humans ruined it. We could drive many miles between homes with just the natural growth between.

Once in a while, we would see where an herb hunter had taken a six-inch square of bark from a cascara tree. Some men made a living by gathering ginseng and other herbs. When we first got there, the kids got acquainted with the local kids as Fanny and I did with the grown folks. They were all very friendly and treated us like they just couldn't do enough for us. Four or five of the kids came to play with our kids one day and asked them to go for a hike in the wooded area across from our place. They were gone a couple of hours, and about three hours after they were home, they were all fighting for turns in the bathroom. The native kids had got our kids to try chewing little pieces of the cascara bark they had peeled from the tree just for a joke. Well, it worked as they had intended it to, but I'm sure Fanny was not very pleased with their joke as she had an extra amount of washing to do.

On the beach in Oregon

On many weekends, we drove about four miles south down Route 101 to a place on the beach where there were sand dunes that were thirty-five feet high for miles along the beach. The only place in sight was a coast guard station about one mile north of where we liked to have our picnic and spend the day. Fanny and I would walk up and down the beach and in and out of the water when the weather was calm. There were dozens of jelly fish swimming in the shallows, and many more were washed up on the beach and everyone had beautiful color designs on their backs, and I don't remember of ever seeing any two of them alike. As many days that we spent there, we never saw a bit of rubbish or even a footprint in the sand. The nearest town or settlement was Winchester Bay. I wonder what is there now in the year 2001.

The Pacific Ocean was beautiful when calm but a terror when it was rough. It rained a lot along that coastal mountain range, but unless it rained real hard, folks there just didn't pay any mind to it and kept on working in it.

Oregon's Beautiful Coast

Courtney was real good to me and took me up to a friend's ranch in the mountains and showed me around. He told me that when their freezer got low in food that all they had to do was sit in a doorway of the horse barn with a gun around ten at night when the deer came past on a trail they used every night. He took me in a room in back of the house where they had two large freezers where they stored enough food to last them through times when they couldn't get up and down the mountain in bad weather even in a Jeep. I understood, on account of the struggle for my Plymouth, to make it up there when the road was dry and no snow. Before I started back home that evening, Courtney took four packages of deer meat from a freezer and gave it to me to take home.

When I was eight or nine years old living at the Wood place, Burt and I and the Yeager boys used to catch big old suckers that would be along the banks of Duck Creek. They looked like they were sleeping as they were so still. We would take a fine copper wire and put about a ten-inch loop with a slipknot so it would act like a lariat and fasten it to a stick a couple of feet long and carefully slip it over the fish from the front to about midway of the sucker and give a quick jerk and you would have that old sucker lassoed.

But when I tried fishing in Oregon for trout, it was altogether different as they were awful smart. They would actually tease me. I could stand on a rock, and those big old brown trout would swim around in about two feet of clear water and let me dangle bait in front of them and bump it with their nose two or three times and glide away and leave me wondering what I was doing wrong. An old Oregonian happened by one day and saw me and asked if I could see the fish, and I said yes, but they won't bite today. He said they never do bite when you can see them because they can see you. Well, I said that I used to catch suckers when I could see them, and that old guy said, "Young man, you are on the sucker end of the pole when you fish that way for trout." The story of my life, I'm always after things from the wrong way.

There is another thing I learned about nature that I suppose most everybody but me knew about, but while we were in Eugene, Courtney asked me one day if I would I like to go black bear hunting with him. He said the bears were feeding in the huckleberry bogs and their meat was good to eat while feeding on berries, but when feeding on fish, it wasn't fit to eat. But I didn't want to go and kill one because when I was a kid, about seven years old, Burt and I were over at Granddad Kennedy's at the Center of the World (the junction of Route 5 and Denman Road). We saw a couple of covered wagons driven by men who were dressed in bright-colored shirts that looked like silk and real baggy pants that looked silky also. There were a couple of women holding babies and three or four larger kids sitting on the seats. Some were riding on the tailgate of the wagon, all dressed in real bright colors.

The men wore big hats, but the women just had old bright-colored rags tied on their head. The strangest thing was they were leading a cow with a calf running along beside it at the back of the front wagon, and stranger yet, the second wagon had a big black bear following it tied by a chain. Route 5, as well as all roads outside the city limits at that time, was just plain old dirt. Some of the main ones were brick or stone, and a few were cinders or gravel, but this one was dirt. After the excitement of seeing those people and their wagons and that bear, Burt and I went over to Route 5 and watched that bear till it was out of sight. Then we noticed in the half inch of dust the bears footprints and tried our footprints with the bears, and by golly, they were almost the same, but the bear's tracks were a little larger than ours. So I guess that is the reason I didn't want to go shooting at anything that so resembled a human.

When deer season came in, Courtney asked me to go hunting with him and a friend, but I had made up my mind that I would have to take Fanny back home to Ohio. She was awful homesick and was crying a lot when she thought no one could see her, and she was worried because Phyllis was due to have a baby, and her dad was sick and kept writing her, wanting her to come back. That kept her all nerved up and feeling bad.

There were twenty-three workers on that housing job. Most were local men, eight were carpenters, but only two of them were local. The rest were from Eugene. They built a tar paper shack for the ones from out of town to sleep and live in while working there. Out of the twenty-three, only six came to work the first day of deer season. A buddy and I were the carpenter gang that day. One of the men who worked that day told the hunters if they got a deer and didn't use the hide that he would like to have one for a car robe.

I gave Courtney a week's notice and reluctantly packed up and left the next weekend for Rosemead, California, to visit with Kitchens before heading back home to Ohio.

We went from Reedsport East to old Route 5, then south to the pretty town of Grants Pass. We left the truck and trailer and drove the car west along the Rogue River to Route 101 and then south through Eureka and the Redwood Forest where we saw those great trees. It was a great sight to see one of God's wonderful creations—those great giants. I hope us greedy humans will leave them for future folks to enjoy seeing. The coast road was a challenge to drive on as it followed the mountain range and had endless hairpin curves without guardrails. It was scary to drive on those high mountainsides. I did have a knob on the steering wheel, which a man at a gas station in Grants Pass told me I should get going on that road. It sure was a help on those curves. We spent the day in the forest, then went back to the trailer and truck and started south the next day.

Jack, Jim, and Fanny Dale in the Redwood Forest

I had a couple of near disasters on the way down to Los Angeles. First, we were going down a steep hill, and a big cattle truck I was following stopped dead still in front of me, and although I was one hundred feet behind him, I had to slam on the electric brakes on the trailer and truck brakes. The trailer brakes caught first and twisted the angle iron hitch so bad that the knob was almost out of the socket. We were a long way from any habitation of any kind, so I had to be real careful driving for the next twenty or so miles. But we got to a small town, and they had to heat the angle iron to straighten it out. Another scare over with!

As we were entering Fresno, California, I got in a bind as we were leaving a side road where we had parked overnight. We were stopped by a traffic light under a railroad overpass, and the approach was up a real steep grade to the main highway. When I tried to start the truck up the hill, it didn't have enough power to get up that steep place unless I had enough room to jack knife it. But the car behind me was a young guy who was reluctant to back up. So we sat there for about fifteen minutes until a man who was in the back came up and explained to that dumbass what I had to do to get started. That little thirty-four-ton Dodge truck was way overloaded as I had over the load limit on it, plus pulling the trailer, which was weighed with all our belongings. In all, about three and a half tons.

We passed the Los Angeles city limits sign at 1:30 p.m., and I thought we would be at Kitchens' place in just a little while, but at 8:30 p.m., I was still hunting for Rio Hondo Street and so tired that I had to do something to rest. I saw a No Parking sign at the side of the street, and I figured if a cop came by, he would either help me or arrest me, and at that point, I didn't give a damn which. But we sat there about twenty minutes, and no one showed up. Then I saw a light in a house window across the street, so I asked one of the kids to go over and ask them if they could tell us where we were and if we could call Kitchens on their phone. He asked what their name was, and when they told him, he said that he had repaired a TV for people by that name on Rio Hondo Street just a couple of days before. So he called them and told Lawrence where we were, and they came to where we were in about ten minutes. Well, we were just around the block from where they lived but were headed in the wrong direction and had to go about five or six blocks farther to a place to get turned around and then get parked for the night. Just to be out of that truck and relax was a real treat!

After spending one day in Los Angeles, I decided that was the last place that I wanted any part of even though it was called the Sunshine State. Well, I think I ran across the dumbest and most ignorant people on this earth there. Everyone I asked about directions either didn't know where they lived themselves or gave the wrong directions. One told me to go to the third light and turn left and go to the end of that street and turn right. Well, it was a very narrow street and up a hill. I went about a mile and came to a barricade with a sign that said dead end. That sign was right because I looked over the barricade, and there was a six-lane freeway about one hundred feet below. I was on that narrow road and no way to go but to turn around. Every home had a hedge along the front of their yards, except for their driveways. So I had to back that forty-two-foot trailer into a driveway opening while sitting uphill. It was a real problem, but I made it, and it only cost me $7 for the shrubs that I ran over.

We headed east on old Route 66. We had a few things that were sort of interesting at the time. I noticed as we were approaching a few miles from Flagstaff, Arizona, that my truck seemed to be real lazy or awful tired because it was having a hard time when we were going downhill for several miles. I started to worry about that old truck not lasting until we got back home to Ohio. I even spoke to the two boys about it. I even reached out the window and slapped the side of the door. I thought the old truck was just getting like I am now; I just fall asleep so easy. Then I looked in the rearview mirror and it looked like we were going uphill instead of down.

The next incident that was new to me was a dust storm, or rather a mud storm, as it started to rain hard along with the dust and wind. It caught us just as we were passing through Albuquerque, New Mexico. The mud, about as thick as gravy, just poured over everything. It was impossible to see anything, so I eased the truck to what I thought was far enough off the road and stopped. Fanny was right behind me; it was a good thing that we were staying close together through towns. We had a hell of a hard time getting that mud off everything.

We had a scare in Oklahoma when passing through the foot-hills. Route 66 was a much used bus route at that time, and as my top speed was forty-five miles per hour, it seemed to me that a bus passed me about every half hour. They would slow down and run alongside for a few seconds and then speed up and pull away, without having that suction effect of two flat surfaces passing each other, and of course, most of the bus drivers knew to do that.

But one smart-ass guy tried passing me at a place where the berm of the road was very narrow, and he was on the outside of the hillside where it was a long way down if he went over the berm. He was going at a higher speed than any other buses that passed us, so although I crowded the bank on my right, he was pulling me toward the bus, and if I had not jammed my brakes on, we would all have gone over the edge. I was a real scared man, and I'm sure that dumb bus driver was also.

We also stopped in Arizona to see the Painted Desert and the south end of the Grand Canyon. The two boys ran way down, about a mile, and explored the small part of the Petrified Forest, and I was sort of bothered as they were bringing a couple of large pieces of the petrified wood with them. Fanny and I bought several small pieces of wood, and I bought Fanny a silver bracelet with a wood setting, and Fanny got me a ring with the same pattern, and I have it on me now, and it has never been off my finger, only to clean it, in almost fifty years. There will never be enough gold in the world to buy it.

There was one other thing that happened on our way home, and that was our last blown-out tire. That was about three hundred miles from home, so that wasn't too bad. It was one of the retreads I had put on before we left Ohio. We had five other tires that I bought before leaving Ohio.

Well, we got back home to Ohio in the late fall of 1953. We found things in about the same shape as when we left with just a few exceptions. The bathroom floor was screwed up; they had left the water tank on the toilet run over, and the tile was all turned up. I guess that I didn't mention this before, but we rented the house to an Army major who was stationed at the depot. We left it partly furnished. He bought an electric kitchen range from Sears and said he would leave it for rent he owed. But in about a week after they had moved to California, a man from Sears came to the house and said the stove was not paid for and, to keep it, we would have to pay them $359. So much for career military men!

Queenie welcomes me home from Oregon.

We used the first several days after getting home just working at fixing things and getting the place arranged to suit us. Then I went to work with Burt. He had two jobs underway. A house and a youth and Sunday school building for the Methodist Church in Braceville. Burt, Ed Kibler, and I were remodeling Chets Market when we left for Oregon. When I got back, Burt had hired Lamarr Senne, and we four worked together for quite a while until work slowed down and Lamarr had a chance to get into Packard Electric. I told him I thought that it would be in his best interest to take that offer on account of the benefits he would get, and I didn't think he was happy with his present job.

I had a good reputation with the Western Reserve Lumber Company and the other building material suppliers, and they sent me a lot of jobs. I guess it was because I always kept my bills paid to date. I made it a rule after losing my home during the Depression to never buy anything unless I knew where the money was to pay for it. That is the reason I hate credit cards and deal in cash wherever possible. I did go into Sears a couple of years ago, and they had a sale on most items if you would use one of their credit cards. Well, after the clerk telling how much I could save with one of their cards, I agreed to take one, but when I got home, I wrote out a check for the bill and put it in the mailbox. Then I took the scissors and cut up the card. Maybe not too smart, but I don't owe them any money.

A fellow stopped at the house one day and asked me if I would be interested in building him a duplex house. I said yes, that we would be interested in building any old kind of house. The man's name was Harry Leadbetter; he was a very interesting guy, but a little hard to understand. A very dry humorist, I just kind of went along with him or humored him until we got a contract signed. I really wasn't surprised when, on the first day we were on the job, the mason who was just loading his tools after he had finished said he was glad he was done with that job. He said, "That's the meanest man I've ever worked for," meaning Harry.

Well, at lunchtime, Harry and his wife drove in the driveway, and the Mrs. Spoke to us, but Harry just walked past us. He had a real grouchy look on his face and never said a word, and neither did we. The next day, we had the subfloor on and were setting down eating our lunch when Harry stopped by. Still wearing that grouch and was walking past us without speaking and it pissed me off. So I jumped up in front of him and said to him, "Harry, this is not Halloween, so take that grouchy mask off your face or else don't ever come here while we are working." Well, he actually smiled and turned around and left. Burt said that I shouldn't have said that to him. Well, I guess I'm just a big mouth, but it really put a smile on a sour face.

Harry smoked a pipe when his wife was near but chewed tobacco when she wasn't around. He would come out to the job every day and check on the progress of the house. And almost every day, he would push a pack of tobacco in my hip pocket so he wouldn't have to carry it. He said he had forgot and left a pack in his pocket and his wife found it and gave him hell. Harry was superintendent of bricklayers at Copperweld Steel. We became good friends, and he was always a very generous person to work for. We did some extra jobs for him after the contract was completed. There was a large stoop at the front of the lower apartment with a deck that had a flat roof. The roof was on the same level as the garage roof, and they wanted to use both as they were flat. They wanted to use them as a porch with a railing and a door to the second floor and a stairway from the ground level.

Harry had heard of canvas laid on white lead painted with aluminum for a deck cover, so he ordered it from an awning company. It turned out to be real good to our surprise. I saw the house several years later, and it was still looking okay then.

In the fifties, I was pretty ambitious and the kids were getting to be teenagers. I started to think of ways to keep them from running wild as some kids with too much time to idle away were on drugs because that is the era when we started to hear about drugs, street gangs, etc., more than ever before. So Archer and Jack were teenagers and getting into the car stage of life for boys, and they were slanting their thoughts toward cars as all teenagers do. I know because I was one of them about seventy-seven years ago. We talked it over, and a gas station north of the driveway seemed to be a logical answer. So we built a building and started into the gas service business. For a while, the boys were interested in it, and after a while, it became an awful sore and weary job, and there were arguments on whose turn it was to tend to it. I worked every day, so it became Fanny's job to take over until I got home, and then as overworked as she was, Fanny had to get meals with some help from the girls.

I had resigned from the Lordstown Volunteer Fire Department when we went to Oregon. The fellows in the department gave me a very nice watch as a parting gift. I must say that I enjoyed my years with the department. It was quite a relief to be rid of the responsibility of chief as it was awfully hard to give all the time that it required away from family and friends. I had worked twenty-four hours every other day at the ordinance depot and eight to ten hours every other day at the building trade, so I was getting tired. It also gave me more time to try to do things to prepare for future years. Until then, I had been struggling to just keep living day to day. So one day, I decided to take a fling at a larger project. I had heard through a grapevine that General Motors was planning a big Chevrolet plant in a nearby area, so I looked and listened around to see if I could find a farm or piece of land for sale that would be suitable for a housing development.

Lordstown was a township five miles square and only had a population of less than four hundred people—in fact just a little over three hundred people—two churches, one school for grades one to twelve, one grocery store, one gas station, a welding business, a thirty-man volunteer fire department, two slaughterhouses, a township clerk and three trustees, about three dozen farmers, and, in those days, two railroads.

I was at Chet Phillips grocery store one day and mentioned to Chet of my thought of buying some property to develop. I thought our kids were growing up and moving away from the farm and going to other places to live. This left some of the farms with just the older folks to work them, and a couple were vacated and left to just go backward. I said I'd like to try to induce some of our kids to have their homes in our area by offering modern homes for them to buy if they were interested. And it might be a help to our own families. Well, Chet was all for that and said he would like to be a part of such a project and would ask around to see if any suitable property was for sale. So that's how Lordstown Realty Inc. got started. It lasted nine years.

We appointed officers. I was president, Ernest Helmich was secretary-treasurer, and Chester Phillips, Floyd Jones, and Lamarr Senne were shareholders. It turned out that Ernie and I got the honor of doing 98 percent of the work aside from the mouth work of organizing Lordstown Realty with suggestions from the shareholders. Floyd did his share of work while he was in the area before he went to Florida to live. I looked after his share after he moved. We had a pretty good young attorney named Charles Atkinson who was a big help to us and helped keep Chet and Lamarr in check as they sure were eager to get into a big-money deal right quick, and that never happened. But old Ernie was a real good and honest guy and was always willing and ready to help with the many projects we had on that farm. We bought a 176-acre farm that had frontage on Salts Springs Road and also on Tod Avenue.

The house on the farm had ten rooms with five fireplaces, one bathroom, five bedrooms, a dining room, a sitting room or parlor, and a big kitchen. With only one bathroom, I reckoned they must have had several chamber pots to take care of the night duties.

The house was built in the 1880s by the Woodward family, which was one of very prominent families in the area at that time. I found a diary written by Henry Woodward while I was doing some remodeling on the upper floor of the house. It was of the 1880s and told of his being a professor at Oberlin College. He had a grandniece who was studying to be an opera singer. Coincidentally, I had done some work on her house for her in the '40s. He also wrote of some of the social affairs of those days. One that was mentioned often were the oyster suppers with the Wilsons, another prominent family in the Lordstown area. Burt Wilson was a medical doctor and Leonard Wilson was a mechanical engineer. I went to school with Doc's son, James, and his wife, Enola, in 1926.

We decided to remodel the big house into a duplex as it was too big to rent as a one-family dwelling. It had a coal furnace in the basement with a thirty-inch firebox that could eat coal and wood as fast as a guy could run up and down those damn steps. We lived in one part of the duplex while we continued to remodel the other part. That house was so cold; even with the furnace stoked for the night, it froze a washcloth that was hung on the side of the bathtub. There were very few early-morning baths taken in zero weather. Well, we decided that to make the place livable, we put in two oil furnaces, insulated the outside walls, put a tile floor in the kitchen, built knotty pine cupboards in the upstairs duplex, painted woodwork, wallpapered walls where needed, and moved upstairs, and then we started remodeling the downstairs. The well water was not very good, so we hired Jim Chuck from Newton Falls to drill a new well. Then we lathed the old summer kitchen that was attached to the kitchen, and Floyd plastered it before he took off to Florida to live. That room held three double beds with plenty of room for dressers and was a good place for boys or girls.

It was a cool house in the summer but took lots of fuel to heat in the winter. It had eleven-foot ceilings downstairs and nine-foot ceilings in the upstairs. It had a seven-foot high attic with a ladder to go through a trap door to a ten-foot square flat metal covered patio with a three foot ornamental iron railing around it. A great place to sit on a warm evening and see the surrounding area and the sunsets. We also saw deer and other wildlife that come out to feed at night.

To begin with, that farm belonged to Mabel Woodward Shively, the wife of Floyd Shively who, at that time, was owner of the Ford Auto Agency in Niles and, in former years, farmed a good sized dairy farm. At the time, we got interested in the farm there was a family who had a dairy of their own and rented the farm from the Shivelys who had moved to Niles. The Shively agency needed a little extra cash. I never did know why, but Floyd told the renter that he wanted to sell the farm, and he could have first chance to buy it. But I guess the man found a better rental deal, so he turned Shively's offer down. Well, I heard of it through the grapevine and went to see Shively, and I guess he was in need of a cash deal real quick, so he quoted me a price I thought was very reasonable. But it had to be cash!

Well, now, that was a hell of a lot of loot for a poor old guy like I was. I was always used to working on a shoestring, and I was full of piss and vinegar, so I took to the road to try and round up some dough. Well, I was a bit surprised, but I was able to corral enough willing money, so it was only a couple of days until we were able to deliver the check for Shively's full purchase price. Chet had talked to his uncle Ernie Helmich and Chet's mother-in-law, Grandma Shirran, and she told him that she would loan him some money, but she would have to do the same for Lamarr, her other son-in-law. So we had six out of seven. I had already asked my brother Burt, but he wasn't in favor of it. I talked to my brother Floyd who was to move to Florida in a short while, but I knew he and Clara were a bit more for a gamble, and Clara came out the next day with a check for the seventh share. Grandma Shirran bought a lot and had us build a house for her on speculation, and it sold before it was completed.

General Motors had bought eight farms shortly after we bought the Shively farm. They had 1,350 acres adjacent to us and sold a fifty-foot right-of-way next to us, but I think it was just one of the dirty little tricks used by big companies and politicians use to cut the other guy out. Their motto is not live and let live, but kill and go to confession. Well, the Pennsylvania railroad cut through the opposite side of the hill from us and put their spur to the GM plant, which was good for us. Then later, through the courts, the B & O railroad put a spur in front, across from the depot crossing Lyntz and Saltsprings Roads, so those smart-ass Penn Railroads paid taxes for forty years on a piece of land that was worthless to them, then sold the front to Ballentines for $1. A great deal!

Adjacent to the southern part of the Lordstown Realty's property at the top of the hill on Route 45, there was a house that was built in the 1840s and used for a stagecoach stop. Most of the old house was much the same in the twentieth century as it was when it was built. There was a lot of hand-chiseled and carved sandstone, such as a stone sink, in the pantry and two stone watering troughs, one inside the yard and one in the barnyard. The fence corners and the gate posts were also of stone.

The Ford family was the only occupants of the old stagecoach house that I can remember. They had a dairy and farmed about 150 acres. Enola, a daughter, went to Lordstown school when I did. She later married Jimmy Wilson, the son of Doc Wilson and a classmate of mine. The Wilsons lived on the eastern side of the top of the hill. They had a fruit and dairy farm across the road from the Fords' dairy farm. The Wilson farm had a big stone watering trough that was fed by a saltwater spring where we counted as many as fourteen deer at one time that came to drink. Fanny and I saw a pure white fawn with a doe and big buck grazing in our backyard one day before GM built their plant and things were at a more natural stage than today.

Now there are two big water towers in front of where the old stagecoach house stood. Before GM bought their farm, the old barn had burned down and they tore the old house down, so all that was left were the two stone water troughs and the old stone sink. They broke all but the sink, so I went and put a chain around it and dragged it down to the side of our house and used it for a birdbath and feeding station.

We had surveyors survey the farm and also eleven-hundred-feet-by-five-hundred depth along Saltsprings Road, giving us twenty-three nice lots with one hundred feet of frontage. And we had three streets laid out.

We rented the pasture on the farm with no charge in order to keep the brush and weeds from taking over. We first rented to Randall Young, who put in fifty or so head of Holstein heifers. Then good-hearted Chet told Jim Kistler, who lived on Saltsprings Road, that he could put a stud pony in the pasture also. It is against the law in Ohio, but of course, Chet, being ignorant of the law and Kistler being the sneaky tight guy that he was, thought he could get away with it, and he didn't care if he got in trouble over it. None of the rest of us knew about it being in there until, one day, Chet's son Jimmy came up to play with our son Jim. They were about eleven or twelve years old and liked to ride their bicycles down the cow trails. They were well-worn paths because it had been a large dairy farm until that time.

Well, the kids just got about fifty yards through the gate at the barn when that big pony stud came charging at them. Of course, the boys were scared and dropped their bikes and climbed through the fence. That stud reared up on his hind legs and pawed the air like a boxer, then grabbed one of the bikes by the front tire and picked it up and whirled it around while standing on his hind legs. I had just driven in from work and saw the whole show, and I went down to Bea and Chet's store and told them to have Kistler to get his damn stud out of that pasture that day or it would be dead in the morning. And I told them they were not to give anyone rights that had anything to do with the farm unless he wanted to buy my share out. Well, I told Ernie and he said he felt the same way I did. We got along pretty good after that for a while.

We dug a large septic tank at a location close to where the GM plant was going to put their sewer line to Warren so people buying lots in the allotment would not have to install septic tanks.

We sold all the lots but six within a year, and each one of the four stockholders got one lot each as first payment on their investment, and I bought one later to build a house on as an investment. Lordstown Realty built two houses, one on Saltsprings Road for Grandma Shirran, Chet's mother-in-law. And we built one on Chester Avenue. Then I got done with trying to do two people's jobs and decided to go back to working for myself again as I had people who wanted me to build houses for them.

I also wanted to build a house for Fanny and the kids and myself on my lot on Route 45 at the southeast corner of the farm.

Kay and Bruce live there now. I was building it in my spare time while working five days a week building other people's homes. I had a good guy named Jimmy Boyett who helped me. He was at our door every Saturday and Sunday from the time the cellar was dug until the house was ready to move into, October 8 to April 14. We did all the masonry, carpentry, plumbing, electrical, painting, concrete, except for the soil stack, fuse box and service, and the concrete finishing, which Al Lutz did. He was another good friend who is gone now.

Around a year later, Chet decided to expand a little, so he made a deal with Lordstown Realty to buy the lot at the northeast side of the farm. It was three lots south of the corner of the village where his store was then. In the early days, when I was in school there, it was just a two-story house with a large dining room where they featured weekly chicken dinners. The front corner was the Abe Deumberger Grocery with an old church pew along the front wall and a pot-bellied coal or woodstove near it. There was about twelve feet of shelves and a seven-foot showcase and several barrels and a couple of wooden buckets sitting on the floor, all in that little room. That was Lordstown's grocery store until 1947, the year Bea and Chet Phillips took over and doubled the size.

After I had gone back to working by myself, I had to just pick up temporary help for a while until Archer decided that he would like working along with me, so I bought fifteen acres on Lyntz Road across from the old Frank Kreitler Dairy Farm. I laid it out in lots with one-hundred-feet frontage on Lyntz Road. There were fourteen lots, so they were real deep. I was getting tired and just did not want to go through the hassle of putting in streets. So I just sold all but one lot that I built on to keep the boys working. We sold the house to Jim and Barb, who needed a larger home at the time. A little later, Archer and Connie bought one of the lots and built on it, and then after Fanny and I went to Florida, they bought another lot and built on it also. Jim and Barb later sold their house and moved to Texas.

I went ahead with the times the way I saw them even if right or wrong, which was of the latter a lot, I guess.

Building slowed down in the early sixties, and Burt had a chance to go to work with a young guy in Cortland named Ellis Mellott, and

Ed Kibler was getting a bit hard to get along with, so I made up my mind to do it alone. Bob was out of a job, so I told him that he could work with me. At that time, I had taken a contract with the Aubrey Tottens to build a house on Route 305 in Cortland, and it is one of the nicest houses for two very nice people that I ever met. We have remained friends ever since. Well, Bob just wasn't very happy at the carpenter trade; he had always liked machinery and was interested in electrical business, so when Tottens' house was framed in and ready for plaster, Bob decided to go to Florida and work at the electrical trade. Johnny Kean and Ilene had gone down there a year or so before and told Bob how nice it was, and that work was plentiful there. So I was left alone to finish Tottens' house. And I was happy to be able to work for folks who let me do my work my way instead of the way some book taught architect would do it. I am proud of that house, and I know Aub and Mary are also.

Going back to when Burt, Ed Kibler, and I were working together; we built a house for Charles (Bus) and Linnabell Mathews in Lordstown. We also did some remodeling on Chet's store and built a house on Palmyra Road for Bus's oldest brother, George, and Ruth Mathews. George and Ruth became two of the best friends that I ever had, and I'm also proud of the house I built for them. It was the second of the three houses that I built for the Mathews brothers. The third was for Al Mathews on North Tod and my son, Archer, built a nice house for Joe and Ilene Mathews on Dodge Street in Warren after I retired and moved to Florida.

George and I went fishing many times together at Mosquito Lake, Lake Milton, Berlin Lake, Lake Nippissing (Ontario, Canada), and Lake Istapoga in Florida. When he and Ruth visited us in Florida, we went to a rodeo, and every year, when they visited us, we went to the Cat House in Sebring for coffee and a large slice of carrot cake for .75 cents. A refill of coffee was free. Whoever said Cat Houses weren't reasonable, and the cake and coffee were both excellent.

To continue on with the building trade, I got pretty disgusted with contracting because of the way things were changing after the wars were over. Prices went up and quality went down. The big cause was like the auto industry advertising is today—promising a lot and giving less. Unless you were willing to cheat a little, or a lot, it was almost impossible to keep going and break even. So I had a chance to get out of it while I still had my head above water. I went to work for the fellow Burt and Ed Kibler were working for. Later, Archer and Jack went to work for Ellis.

Archer and I worked together until one Saturday when I had a heart attack. While working extra time to complete a job for a young couple who were going to have a new addition to their family and were very impatient to have the house ready by the time it arrived, I had sharp pains in my chest all day. I thought it was just another ache, but I was wrong again, as I usually am. I went home and cleaned up, ate supper, and, twenty minutes later, started to have real hard pains and threw up; them damn pains got to be too much for me, and I told Fanny I guessed that I had better get some help. So we got in the car and Fanny pushed that old buggy the fastest it ever went until we got to the Penn Railroad on Market Street, and there was a train stopped across the tracks. I was in so much misery then that I asked Fanny if she would get out of the car and let it roll ahead into the train. But of course, she didn't. I don't know how long it took because I was out of it until we were in the hospital with the doctor and nurses asking questions. They decided that I had a heart attack. Dr. Lewis was my doctor at the time, and I served my time in there under his care.

The Wilsons were real good neighbors and did a lot of nice things for me while I was recovering from my heart attack. Jim and Enola brought us all kinds of fruit from their orchards. When I was able to do a little work in my shop, they brought me many kinds of dry fruitwood to turn on my lathe to make various wooden sconces, toadstools, shelves, candleholders, etc. Enola even took a lot of the items up and sold them at their fruit stand.

Florida and Retirement

AFTER THE HEART ATTACK, Archer took over the building business. The doctor told me that I should not stay in a cold climate another winter with my heart problem and suggested I go to a warmer place for at least the cold months. So we thought we would try Florida as Floyd and Clara were down there and seemed satisfied.

Kay and Bruce rented our place as we decided not to sell until we were sure that we could find a place to live and be satisfied away from the kids. Also, Barbara's mother and dad, Mary and John Kline, had moved to Avon Park a year or so before, and John had died just a month after they had bought a home and got settled there.

I had told my cousin Edna Archer that we were planning on going to Florida to visit and look around for a place to live in the area where Floyd and another cousin, Georgia Villers, lived. Edna's husband, Charles, had passed away a couple of years previous, and Edna was wanting to get away from the house for a spell, she said. She asked me if she could ride along with us. After consulting Charlie about it, he said it was good idea. So I asked Fanny if she cared to have Edna go with us, and she said okay, that she thought Edna would be good company for us as she always seemed to be a jolly person.

A few days before we started out, I was just starting with a mild bladder problem, but I didn't think it was a serious thing. But after about an hour into the trip, I started to look for a gas station to relieve my bladder. Well, Edna decided to go at that time also, but when I got back out to the car, Edna was not out for ten more minutes. We were only on the road a few more miles until my old water system was yelling at me again to hunt another gas station, and I found one just in time to avoid a wet pair of trousers. Edna had to get out also. Well, from then on, it was the same deal every time we stopped, which was about every other gas station we went by on that whole trip.

What started out as a trip of joy was a real humdinger. There was one bit of amusement by our one and only Edna. We had stopped at a gas station in South Carolina, and after getting back into the car after fulfilling my duty inside and then waiting fifteen minutes on the women, Fanny came out and told me that Edna was stuck in a commode. The man who tended the gas station had sent for his wife who lived nearby to come and help that dingbat out. All those stops, I really do not think she really needed to go but was just curious about who knows what. And evidently, she never did learn not to sit on a commode without making sure the seat was down.

Well, the bladder infection got a pretty good hold on me before we got to the Boynton Beach area where Floyd lived. And the trip took much longer than we had planned. But fortunately, Fanny and Mary Kline had talked by phone the day before we left Ohio, and as our route to Boynton went through Avon Park where Mary lived, Fanny promised Mary that we would stop in for a short visit. I was about out of it when we got to Mary's place and couldn't even remember driving into her driveway. I was in bad shape that night with a fever and fell in the bathroom and cut my head open on the corner of the vanity. Next morning, Fanny took me to Dr. Ostling in Avon Park, and he sent me straight to the hospital with a fever of 104. I was there for ten days. In that time, Floyd and Clara came up from Boynton and took Edna down to their place. So my introduction to Florida life was spent in Walker Memorial Hospital. Fanny stayed with Mary Kline while I was in the hospital, and they spent quite a lot of their time in Mary's free hours from work, looking around the north highlands county area and looking for a house that Fanny would be pleased with. She had made up her mind that she would not be satisfied in the Boynton area, and I think she was wise as I found out later that the Sebring area was much more to our liking for a home.

Fanny found a little house on Hibiscus Street in Sebring, just south of Avon Park, that wasn't quite finished yet but would be completed in about ten days, so we went to Floyd and Clara's and stayed until the house was ready. In the meantime, Clara and Fanny shopped for things to furnish the house with, and I helped Floyd. Then Fanny, Clara, and I took one of Floyd's trucks and hauled the stuff up to Sebring, and we moved into our new home.

Vic Mellooepsa was our neighbor on one side and Floyd Higden and his wife lived on the other side, all nice people. In fact, it was a nice neighborhood. I spent the first couple of weeks helping Fanny get the house organized and working on the outside, getting the lawn and shrubs planted. Then I put up a metal shed. After that, we drove back to Ohio to get my boat and our TV and other stuff. Bruce and Kay drove the truck, and Archer, Fanny, and I went in the car.

Old Vic and his wife were good neighbors, and we remained in touch as long as Vic lived, which was just one week shy of his one hundredth birthday. Mrs. Vic was a kindly lady who was only about the size of a ten-year-old and Vic was 6 foot 2 and tipped the scales at about 290. Fanny and I got along fine with them and played a lot of cards with them. Whenever Mrs. Vic would win a game, she would always say, "It's your turn now."

Vic and I went fishing a lot, Vic always wanted to take his boat as it had a top and he couldn't take the hot sun. I would go but got a bit of a fright in my bones as he was a very poor driver. But he insisted on doing the driving until we would (through luck) get to a boat ramp, then he would decide he had to go to the restroom real quick. He would ask me if I would mind backing the boat into the water to save time. I found out later that Vic had a problem with backing up with a trailer, and the man at the dock had to take over for him after he had wrestled with the damned machine for an hour and ended up crosswise with the ramp.

I bought a Wheel Horse riding mower as it was too much for me to push a mower in the sand with my ticker not up to par. One of the neighbors, George and Josephine Marks, and their son, Bob, were a real nice family. Bob was just a bit slow, and I felt sorry for him as I thought his dad, although being good to him in many ways, took advantage of him in some ways. Bob never would call Fanny and I by our first names although Bob was forty-six years old then. We were always Mr. and Mrs. Jones to him. Bob could not get a driver's license, so he never got to drive anything but his bicycle. So when I got the mower, he was right over to see it. He said, "Oh boy, that's a nice machine. I would like to have one." Then he asked me if he could sit on the seat. Fanny ran in the house and got the camera and told Bob to get on the mower and smile for her. He sat on that mower and looked like the proudest guy in town!

Well, old Bobby was over at our place every morning after that until we moved away two and a half years later. I guess Fanny and I missed our kids, so we kinda looked after Bob. He was always wanting to help us do whatever we were doing, but many times, we really could have done better alone. He followed me around when I was mowing until, one day, I let him get on the mower, and so of course, he wanted to mow for me and I let him try it. Well, that was my big mistake although he only ran over two little orange trees and cut off one hibiscus bush. But that wasn't the worst part of the mistake; the worst part was that every morning after, our doorbell would ring about 8:00 a.m. and Bobby would be there and would say, "Mr. Jones, your lawn needs mowing," and we would have to tell him it didn't. He told Fanny and I that he liked to work for us because we didn't holler at him, but his dad did. When Fanny got the pictures back she had taken of him sitting on the tractor, he was so happy and wanted a picture to show his "mover." Then he came back and told us how proud his "muver" was of him and he wished that he had put his new pants on when he had his picture taken.

Bob had a little dog he named Penny, and it was quite often a guest of ours and especially of Fanny's. After we moved to Craig Avenue, the Marks family visited us about every week and always brought Penny with them. She rode on the floor of the rear seat until they turned onto our street, then she would jump up and yip and make a fuss until they let her out of the car. She would run in the house and stand in front of our refrigerator, waiting for Fanny to get her a little piece of cheese. Theo she would go over to Fanny and jump up on her lap and go to sleep. Bob died of cancer when he was fifty-eight years old and was honored by the largest funeral attendance ever held in Sebring. Although Bob was slow in some ways, he was talented in others. He was an exceptionally good piano player and never took a lesson but would listen to a piece played at church, then go home and play it perfectly just from memory. George and Penny died about a year after Bob, but Mrs. Higden, who had a leg amputated, lived a couple years after that.

We didn't have space enough between lots on either side of our place to get my boat into the back without getting on the neighbor's lawn, so we decided to sell my truck so I could at least get the boat on the drive in back of the car. Well, that got to be a pain in the posterior parts, so we decided to look for a place with more space.

So we went space chasing and found a house with an adjoining lot beside it on Craig Avenue, just one street from Lake Sebring. We later bought a lot adjoining our lot on the back that was across the street from a half-acre community park. Me and one other neighbor took care of it. It had a hedge on three sides. It was nice, but only a couple of us men seemed to have fallen heir to the maintenance of it, but there were about twenty families that had access to use it.

The couple we bought the house from were a pair who weren't quite as honest as Old Abe. We had to call them ahead of time before they would show the house, so we assumed they were a working couple, but when we went to see the place, she was baking cookies and had the countertop covered with papers. Only about a third of it showing. I asked for a drink of water after the man told me how good it was, so the old girl got me a nice cold drink from a jug in the refrigerator, and it was good and what we could see of the countertop looked good. We went to an abstract place in Sebring and had all the paperwork done the next day and made arrangements to move in three days since they wanted to move right away. We were real busy getting ready and figured we'd move the fourth day.

The fourth morning when we got there about seven thirty, we found out they had gone the second day and did not let anyone know where. The neighbors said they left in a U-Haul truck in the late evening. We understood why as soon as we stepped into the kitchen door. The countertop on the cupboard was torn and burned where that fine lady had covered it with paper when we were looking to buy. But when I went in the bathroom and flushed the toilet and saw the water, I was really disappointed in my fellow man. I really think we learned a real lesson. That episode taught me a few more words not to be said on Sunday or around most nice folks.

Well, anyway, we did have enough of our own land to park our boat and some extra to park an extra car. I had sold my pickup a month before we had moved from Hibiscus Street, and Ben Wagner, Floyd's father-in-law, had a Dodge car that he was wanting to get rid of, so I got it for pulling my boat and so that Fanny would have a car to drive when I was out fishing. We got rid of it after a while as we had a couple of kids in the area that emptied the gas tank a couple of times. They had been accused of putting sand in gas tanks and just all kinds of destruction to property. So I sold the car to Betty and Jack for the kids to drive to college. We had a screened orchid shed we used for storage. One day, while we were away, those lousy brats ripped one whole side of the screen off. They were kids of working parents; one family lived across the street and the other beside us. Their parents were a telephone executive, a hospital blood technician, a bank secretary, and a schoolteacher. The kids were from eleven to eighteen years old, and they all ran back into a thick grove of pine trees after school each day and had a pot party.

We had two lots on Craig Avenue; one was planted with citrus fruit trees about three years old and not real healthy, but there were seven trees on the house lot which were doing well. There was a nice variety, a Key lime, two Persian limes, a navel orange, a lemon, a tangelo, and a Valencia. The Valencia looked like a Christmas tree the winter it snowed there; it was full of fruits, and little coat of snow let the oranges stick out like Christmas bulbs.

Aubrey and Mary Totten moved down from Cortland that winter after they bought a home on Route 17, three miles from Avon Park and about seven miles North of Sebring. We helped them get acquainted with the ways of the south—that is, as much as I knew, which was not nearly as much as we both learned later. We had a good time anyway; we worked, drank, ate, played cards, and enjoyed ourselves, especially when George and Ruth Mathews visited us. George and I always got up early in the morning, and he would come over to our place, and many times we went up to the Cat House and had a cup of coffee and a piece of their good carrot cake and got back to our place before the other folks were up.

The Tottens went back north every winter, and Fanny and I checked on their place at least once a week, except when we took our short winter vacation. While I was going home from town one day, I was looking at the eyesore entrance to our development and wondered why it was so bad looking and no one seemed to care. So I went over to see a neighbor who had lived there several years, and I was told everyone was waiting on someone else to start the ball rolling. Once someone started, they would join in to help fix it. It had been a brick curved wing wall on a concrete base about twelve feet long on either side, but vandals had played pretty rough climbing on it and pushed it over, and it was just a bunch of scattered bricks.

So Mr. Cunningham, who lived close by, came up to our place one evening and said that he and his wife heard that we were interested in seeing the little park and the entrance fixed up and kept up, and they were willing to help in any way they could. They said they would talk to other folks in the area and stir their pride up a bit, as a feller says wake them up. Some of them did contribute as much as a buck, and others gave a promise as soon as they could borrow some from their babysitter. The Buckinghams and Fanny and I made up 80 percent of the cost and bought mortar and sand and worked three days cleaning the old cement from the brick. We spent four more days putting the walls back up and two days painting them. I put a pointed cap on the walls so the kids couldn't play on them. (I sure am a mean old fart, I guess.)

I also had a couple of days that were interesting while at that place. We had a beautiful naval orange tree, and it was full of extra fruit. George Mathews was there one day and said that he really liked those oranges, so Fanny got him one of those orange juice nipples, and he sure did make use of it. We had a pretty passion flower that was really nice when in bloom.

We had a pet squirrel that we let in the kitchen, and he would crawl up on our lap and let us feed him peanuts. One day, we went to town, and he chewed a hole in the window screen and was on the countertop, eating my peanuts out of the jar. Fanny told me that she wasn't happy about having that animal in the house, so I had to inform that little devil that he wasn't welcome anymore.

I was proud of those nice big navel oranges, but there were several loudmouthed sapsucker woodpeckers that were real fond of them also and would peck holes in them. The ants then went after the juice that bled out of them, then the sapsuckers would come back and eat the ants and squawk their heads off, telling me to go to hell when I would chase them away. Well, being the hotheaded ass that I am, I bought myself a Daisy BB gun. I didn't want to kill them vandals. I just wanted to prove to them that they weren't welcome to that fruit.

I got up one morning when I heard them in that tree, just making their usual racket, so I snuck out the door and put the trusted firepower to my shoulder and squinted down the sights and didn't see a damn thing, so I tried about three more times. Then I shut that eye and could see okay out of my left eye, but not the right. I went into the house and asked Fanny if I still had an eyeball on the right side, and she said I did. I told her that it wasn't behaving right. She didn't think it looked bad, but I went to the eye doctor to make sure that I wasn't clear off my rocker. After he looked in my eye with one of his contraptions, Doc said to me, "You can't see, can you?" He said I had a massive occlusion (a bunch of blown up little blood vessels).

Another darn thing happened while I was painting the laundry room. I was reaching around the water heater and ruptured my right side. It got so bad that it would come out so easy, and I'd have to lie on the couch and put my leg up over the back and push it back in. So Doc said surgery. So that was that. Those were most of my stories of the bad part of Craig Avenue.

Of course, we did have some good memories from that time. We had our card-playing buddies, Jim and Billie Gassaway, and Dr. Lungerhousen and his wife who insisted on having me over for meals at their house every time Fanny was away for one day at a time.

There was another doctor by the name of Botts that lived close who was a buddy of Lungerhousen. One day, the two docs decided to explore an alligator habitat that was across the canal from them at a little lake called Hidden Lake. They found a nest, but old mama gator saw them at the same time and didn't like them old geezers fooling around. She gave a loud grunt and took after those snoopy old docs and took after them. She was a bit faster than they were, so they climbed up a couple of little trees. When he told me the story, Doc said she kept them up there for a long time. Doc was nice to me; he used to send and get flu vaccine and inoculate his wife, himself, a lady neighbor, and me. He was a very kind man. I went over to see him one day, and he had a ladder leaning against a palm tree in the front yard. I said to Doc, "You shouldn't be climbing up in that tree at your age. I can do it for you."

He said, "It's not for me. There's a pet squirrel that's pregnant, and I thought that the ladder would make it easier for her to climb up to her nest."

Fanny and I were in the Cat House one day having lunch when George Forst, a real estate salesman for Gracey McCoy Realty, came in for his morning cup of tea, which he never missed, and came over with a big smile on his face. He said, "Joneses, I've got just the place you've been looking for at a real good price." We told him that we weren't looking for a place.

Well, we didn't have anything special to do that day, so we decided that we would take a look at his gem. We followed him out to the big Lake Istapoga. We had never looked around in that area before. It was just one mile southwest on Route 98 in the Spring Lake area. It was on a canal 200 feet off the lake with one and a half acres of land with 180-foot canal frontage. There was an old seven-room house with three big oak trees in front, five big cypress, three eucalyptus, and two calamondin in the surrounding yard. There was a wire fence surrounding the property. The house was old enough to retire. I would say it was from the 1900 era or older. It had two bedrooms, one and a half baths, a den, dining room, kitchen, and a large utility room. There was a carport building with a garage, workshop, and storage room with a big freezer in it. Fanny liked the old house and the location. She said it was more like her old home on the farm in Ohio. The house was pretty much furnished with rustic furniture, so we were used to that type of thing for most of our lives, so that was no hardship for us. It did have an electric stove, a microwave oven, and a dishwasher. We were able to sell our house on Craig Avenue real quick and we moved in that same month.

We hadn't got the car clear through the road gate until a man came over and introduced himself as Joe Godfrey. He right away offered to help with anything we needed to do. Well, it turned out there were many chores we helped each other with over the years to follow. One thing I did was build a little dock so I could get my boat in the water.

Joe was a native of Florida, born and grew up in Wachulla. He talked with the old Southern brogue and was, at times, a little hard to understand as he talked real fast.

There was a mud one lane road on a thirty-foot right-of-way private road with a cattle pasture on the other side of the road. It grassed one horse, one pony, and four hundred bovines. There was a wild orange tree, two big lemon, and two big grapefruit trees in the wooded area across from our house. There was an abundance of wildlife in that area. Wild turkey, wild pigs, bobcats, rattlesnakes, armadillos, a large variety of birds, kit hawks, big blue heron, limp-kins, pileated woodpeckers, and many more.

I had one special pet (a blue heron) by the name of Oscar that followed me around the yard like a dog waiting for me to catch him a fish, which I did every day that I was home. He would fly to the top of a cypress tree sometimes and squawk at me if I wasn't prompt enough to catch his fish. He always let me know when he was hungry.

Fishing was really great the first seven years we lived there. We used the boat for a short time, then decided that a pontoon would be so much nicer when we had visitors and was handier for us to take care of. It accommodated six people with lawn chairs, and four could fish at one time without being crowded. We took a card table and played cards and took the gas grill and had burgers and hot dogs and had a lot of fun!

We had a lot of visitors in those days. Old neighbors, Vic and Vivian, from Sebring would come every week for a fish fry. The Tottens and Cessnas visited often when they lived in Avon Park. Our kids, other relatives, and many friends from Ohio made frequent trips to see us. George and Dorothy Davis came and stayed ten days, and both said it was the best vacation they ever had. We played cards, fished, drove around to do sightseeing, and talked of our younger days together. We always enjoyed the time we spent with our kids when they visited. And we looked forward to seeing George and Ruth Mathews as we always had enjoyable times when they were with us. Today, most of those good folks have passed on, but I still can remember the good days in my heart and my head.

I had some bad days while we lived there also. I had been having a few angina pains when doing anything strenuous since my heart attack in 1972. By 1979, I was having more problems, so I decided to see a heart doctor. My MD made arrangements for me to go to Orlando Hospital to have a heart catherization. They found a lot of blockage. I had to have quadruple bypass surgery.

Fanny and Floyd stayed up there in a hotel across from the hospital for a week, and then we went back home. I had to have bed rest for about a week. Bob and Betty came and helped Fanny with the chores around the place until I was able to do a little work. While Betty was there, I was awakened one morning by a noise outside my bedroom window. It sounded like something was in a petunia bed under my window. I called to Betty in the next room to see if she had heard the noise. She came and looked out my window and said, "Oh, Dad, it's some animal just ruining your flower bed." Well, I knew right away who the culprits were. Fanny heard us talking and got up and the two women went out to the laundry room and each found a weapon, a mop and a broom, and went to do battle with five armadillos. Well, the women were getting tired, and they didn't seem to be discouraging or even scaring those varmints. While they were standing there, trying to decide what to do, good old neighbor Joe Godfrey came over with a pistol. By the time he got there, the culprits decided they had played enough, so they took off for home across the road. Joe emptied his gun at them, but they continued on down a cow path to safety.

The worst thing that happened while we lived there was when Fanny passed away. If it hadn't been for my kids and a lot of good friends, I don't know what I would have done!

There was a big old live oak tree in the back that had been struck by lightning, and they had cut it up and left the stump. I tried to get rid of it, but it was a real chore to chop it out. It was the hardest wood I have ever seen. I could hardly nick it with an ax, and it was just as hard to burn. I went over in the pasture across the road and cleaned all the brush and anything that would burn from around the trees and even burned several old tires around it, and it still took about a year to get it all burned out. One day, after I had a big bed of red coals beside it, Joe and I were talking. Joe suggested using it to cook our supper. I said how about a catfish meal. He had caught two that morning and had them in the freezer. We wrapped them in tin foil with a chunk of butter and a sprinkle of salt and pepper. In about twenty minutes, we were eating some of the best fish we ever ate. Those old wood coals sure did a job on them.

There was a variety of fish in the canal and lake and a lot of alligators that nested along Bird Creek. There were specks, black bass, pike, shell crackers, bluegills, catfish, and bream. The specks were of nice size and one of my favorites for eating. We used to cook large platters of them when we had company. There were good-size big-mouthed bass that some folks fished for exclusively, but I just plain fished. I usually used artificial bait or minnows but, once in a while, would catch a few shiners and cast for bass, but I caught a pike now and then. Joe and I had ourselves a catfish when we decided on a change. There was a big yellow tomcat that a kindly family that lived up the road apiece from me; he did the neighborly act of moving away and leaving the cat to whoever would take it. Of course, no one was notified of their hospitable act, so poor old tomcat had to hunt some boneheaded person to take care of him. Out of thirteen residents on that road, I guess that I was the one who fell heir to the cat-keeper position. Tom's diet consisted of one or two large shiners. I would get the shiners by making a little ball from bread, putting it on a hook and fish off the dock with old Tom sitting at my side, licking his chops until I pulled in his supper. An act that usually only took from one to three minutes of my valuable time. About that time, old Oscar the blue heron would squawk, and I would have to do the same for him as I had to be nonpartial to those guys.

There are always two sides to most everything in life, and life at Istapoga was in line with the world. I had problems with a good neighbor on the south side of the lot. The first complaint I had from him was voiced one evening when we were playing cards. He said that my putting poison on my fire anthills that I was just driving them over to his place. The next time we were invited to his place to play dominoes, he complained about the Spanish moss that was blowing off my cypress trees onto his place. I guess I should mention this fine gentlemen's name. I don't think Elmer Grove was a bad kind of person; he just had a hard time showing any good qualities. I guess a fella could get along with Elmer if he'd do everything Elmer's way, but I just couldn't quite get acclimated to all of his ways.

So toward the end of my stay, there we quit playing dominoes together, which made me feel bad because I was about the only neighbor he had there. Before I moved away from there, I decided that place was a bit too much for me to take care of, so I had a lot eighty feet wide surveyed off the south side of the property. It happened that the original survey was off a couple of degrees, and the new one put my boundary line over on the Grove property about two and a half feet. Of course, that caused the boundary on all thirteen lots on the road to be off. No one else complained, only Elmer, and he bellowed like a bull and threatened to have me arrested for having that survey done. He yelled and called me every name ever heard of, which didn't do either of us a whole lot of good.

I had a nice little garden in back of the garage and raised some real large turnips and a lot of vegetables and a few flowers. I had several flower beds around the house and along the front fence and a couple of loofah vines that had several dozen sponges on them.

Betty, Jack, and John came out to see us often from Miami Land and Jack and John helped me with chores around the yard and Betty helped Fanny inside. Us guys went fishing a lot and ate our catch also. We made homemade ice cream with chopped fresh peaches one day, and I believe it was about as good as any of us had ever eaten. We sometimes took a deck of cards, a couple of fishing poles, and our lunch on the pontoon out on the lake and trolled around, eating, fishing, and playing cards all at the same time. John stayed with me several times. I would walk out to Route 98 every morning, and most times Joe would walk with me and John when he was there. John would pick a bucket full of calamondin and take them across the road to feed the cattle and watch them eat and slobber. Those little fruits were so sour that although they liked them, the slobbers would be from their mouth to the ground.

When we bought the place from Mrs. Ewing, we were told that the thirty-foot roadway was a private road and it was ours to maintain. Well, Joe and I were the only year-round residents, so we were always stuck with getting shell rock and fixing the road. Some of the winter folks paid a little on the material, but only one or two of those grateful ever mentioned about the labor. We kept fit for our pay.

Ralph and his wife lived next to Joe, and he was our three-hundred-pound mailman (self-appointed, of course). He would hand us our mail one piece at a time and tell us who it was from and if it was a check or hold it up to the light to see if he could read the contents. Quite a guy!

I was very happy there until after Fanny was gone. Then Joe and I were there by ourselves until Joe married a nice lady from Zofa Springs. But for the two years before that, Joe and I just struggled along on our own with a little help from friends now and then. We would exchange samples of our cooking (which we really did a job on sometimes), but we survived anyhow. After Joe got married and I was out there by myself, I got a little calico cat. It was a good little pal. But I decided to get a trailer and put it on the lot next to Elmer. He came back in the spring and really tried to give me a hard time ever time he saw me outside. So between that and some of my family telling me I needed to move someplace with more people close by and the fact that the fishing was getting poor on account of the lake being ruined by hydrilla, and I was having a problem keeping up the work of caring for that big place, I went up to Sebring and bought a mobile home in Whispering Pines mobile park.

I guess before leaving the old place I'd better tell about the worm farm I had. It was an old tractor tire with about a third cut out of it to make a round dish. I filled it halfway with good soil, a handful of newspaper pieces, a cup or so of cornmeal. Then add a cup of fishing worms and dampen with water and let them little suckers go into the act of reproducing and nature will do her thing, and you will have all the worms you need in a short time. Of course I mean worms to fish with. Then it was, "So long, Elmer."

I bought a big double-wide mobile home that was furnished at a fair price. It was a lot more room than I needed, but in a good location.

You may think I'm complaining here, but that's not my intention. There are just too many old widows in retirement villages compared to the male population. Fact is the damn men take off for wherever men go to when they pass on (a nice way of saying *die* but the same results, I understand). Anyhow those poor old gals always are having so many household problems and are not equipped or don't have the know how to correct then. Then it falls on us poor old bachelor guys to take over. "Of course, we are mostly kindhearted old farts and pretend we are more than willing to help." End of quote.

The folks that I bought the place from were a couple of fastidious old farts from up north in Michigan. They had a bit more money than the average mobile park folks have or admit to having when paying for labor to some poor sucker trying to keep up with the grocery bill for his family.

I had a carport, screened room, and laundry room on the ground level and a nice little backyard with two fruit trees and several shade trees. I played cards and shuffleboard, polished wood walls and furniture, cooked, and rode my bike on the back road for recreation. I had good neighbors on both sides, so I didn't get lonesome. Ilene and Johnny had a spot in the park, and Tottens lived in the adjoining park. The Cessnas were in a park close by, but of course, they went back north in the summer. That left me alone in the summer, except when I would take my vacation in the summers. But owning a home is a bit different than renting. It takes a lot of maintenance in the summer in Florida. Everything gets out of control in such a short time.

I really never had very much to bitch about, that is, aside from those damn clowns in Washington. Some of the things they do makes an old square like me go into a tailspin now and then. The senators and congressmen spend a heap of money to get in office, then the big business hires lobbyists to tell those clowns what to do. They can't be trusted because they'll say one thing and turn around and do just the opposite. I sure do wonder about those guys. For example, one of those senators ran for president and didn't make it, gave all he could to get a better man than he was impeached from office on a sex charge. Then not very long after that, he and his wife were praising the great values of Viagra on national TV. I guess, in their minds, it must be a more honorable act to prime the pump with a pill than to just do it a natural way. Anyhow, that deal confused this old fart to no end.

Back to Whispering Pines. We had a lot of enjoyable times in the winter months with Keans, Tottens, Mathews, Cessnas, and a lot of other old friends—and, of course, when my kids could come down. We had holidays and weekends when groups of us would get together and have some pig roasts and other cookouts. Every New Year's Eve, we had a pig roast prepared by Mary Totten, a great cook, and Aubrey always offered a jolly water toast which helped to liven the party a bit.

Then in 1985, I did something that, unfortunately, created a different life for myself. I married a lady named Fran. I shouldn't even say anything about this part of my life because I really think it was something we both would rather forget. Although it wasn't all bad, the way I see it, we just were not meant for each other. I never really felt anything against her, and I really, to this day, feel sorry that we just couldn't find a solution to our differences. So be it.

I was not a faithful church member, but the first year we were together, we went to the Methodist church almost every Sunday. But after I listened to the preacher talk more about money than he did about religion, I decided that I just could not be a dedicated member. I listened to that old warhorse tell people what amount they should give to the church, but I couldn't see as he was giving till it hurt since he had a big new home, an airplane, and a new Olds 98. So I went back to my old oak tree church.

We did have a few good times together. We took a cruise to Cancun and a tour by car to the northeast. We went to Vermont,

New Hampshire, Maine, and Nova Scotia, then down the East Coast, stopping at Warm Springs, to see FDR's little white house and St. Augustine.

Fran got me started playing golf at the age of seventy-five, and I enjoyed it. We played at several courses. In 1987, we built a house at Spring Lake. In 1989, I got my first hole in one and another in 1990. Fran also got one that same year.

As time went on, we just decided things were not working out for us and we should part and go our own ways. In 1995, we parted friendly, and Fran took her belongings and moved to Avon Park. I stayed there at the house for a couple more years.

In 1997, I went down to my brother Floyd's and stayed awhile. While I was there, I went over to help an old friend Grace Mumma with some repairs on her house to get it ready to sell. It had gotten kind of rundown during her husband's terminal illness. There was so much to do there that I rented a room from Grace and traveled back and forth from Lantana to Spring Lake to care for my place and back to Grace's to work on repairs there.

SPRING LAKE -- On May 27, the Ladies of Spring Lake Women's Golf Association played low gross and low net in compatible flights. The winners in A Flight were, low gross at (84) Marlene Whitaker and low net at (78) Peggy Gregory.

In B Flight, low gross went to Fran Jones (101) and low net, Mary Moore (73). In C Flight, the low gross winner was Lee Flintoff (111), and low net was Doris Swan (85).

On Tuesday, May 21, the day's play for the Spring Lake Men's Golf Association was a two best balls of team which was won by the team of Van Kinnamon, Garnet Moore, Richard Reed and Dick Stiving carding a 118 (minus 26) total.

The teams of (1) Jake Goodman, Jack Lamoureaux, Walt Gingrich, Howard Marsh and (2) Warren Kern, Walt Durance, Afton Hensley and Arch Jones tied at 123 (minus 21). There was also a tie at 125 (minus 19) between (1) Al Golden, John Tenuta, Ernie Grossinger, Rod Allan and (2) Sam Martin, Hugh McCartney, Del Wulf and Paul Flintoff.

Spring Lake

On Tuesday, May 28, the Spring Lake Club played a team pro-am game and the team of Al Golden, John Manuel, Jack Gardner and George McMillen won with a score of plus 6 points.

At plus 5 were Larry Maloney, Bob Beeghley, Wayne Fulwider and Stan Wrobel. The threesome of Warren Kern, Doc Decker and Bill Snyder had plus 3, followed by the plus 1 by Sam Martin, Red Bohanon, Bernie Wheeler, and Arch Jones.

Closest to the pin were: Gene Sanford, Doc Decker, Jack Gardner, Bob Shumate, Sam Martin, Jack Gardner (2), Doc Decker (2) and Arch Jones.

Thursday's play was individual pro-am with a plus 7 by Arch Jones winning first place. Following Jones at plus 6 was Van Kinnamon, John Manuel plus 5, Howard Weekley plus 5, Jack Gardner plus 5, Foster Stutsman plus 4, Paul Gillespie plus 3, Red Bohanon plus 3, Wayne Fulwider plus 3, Mike Johnson plus 2, Warren Kern plus 2, Larry Maloney plus 2, Al Golden plus 2, Jim Young plus 2.

Closest to the pin were: Van Kinnamon, Foster Stutsman, Bob Walker, Arch Jones (2), Larry Malonet, John Tenuta and Dudley Clark.

Johnnie Walker. Golf

INTERNATIONAL

HOLE-IN-ONE AWARD

Name ___CHARLES A. JONES___
Course __SPRING LAKE___
Hole ____2ND____ Yardage ___138___
Date ___8/15/91___

Blended Scotch Whisky, 43.4% Alc./Vol. • 1996 Schieffelin & Somerset Co. New York, NY

Authenticated **GOLF DIGEST** HOLE-IN-ONE CLEARING HOUSE

Johnnie Walker. Golf

INTERNATIONAL

HOLE-IN-ONE AWARD

Name __CHARLES JONES___
Course __SPRING LAKE___
Hole __13TH__ Yardage 140
Date __4/16/90___

Blended Scotch Whisky, 43.4% Alc./Vol. • 1996 Schieffelin & Somerset Co. New York, NY

Authenticated **GOLF DIGEST** HOLE-IN-ONE CLEARING HOUSE

I had some special neighbors at Spring Lake—Matt and Mary Silveroli, Hank and Mary Shantz, Gerry and Mike Ferenzio, Ken and Jean Kellog, and many others. Matt was the one that I saw more of as he was either at our house or passed by almost every day going to work at the golf course. We had a lot of armadillos that really caused us a problem with our lawns. Although harmless animals in other ways, they sure could tear up a lawn overnight. We got a box trap and caught at least fifty of them in the nine years I lived there. We also caught at least a dozen each of opossums, raccoon, and one skunk. We took most of them around on the back road and turned them loose in a cattle pasture. We did shoot three of the coons as they acted and looked sick or rabid.

The first year I lived there, I had a couple dozen pineapple plants in part of a garden, and they were doing real well until one morning I went out to find them eaten off at ground level. Rabbits had got to them. So the next time I saw a bunny in the backyard, I got my Daisy air gun thinking I might sting him and scare him off. I shot and couldn't believe what I saw when that little critter did a backward flip and stretched out on its back dead. As many times while hunting in years past, I had shot at rabbits and they just kept on running. I was just dumbfounded. Fran asked me what I was going to do with it, and I told her I would leave it for the big old wildcat that passed across the backyard every morning and evening; he could have it for his breakfast, and by golly, he did.

I also had a big problem with rats. Although we never got any in the house, they would chew holes in the garden vegetables and most everything in the yard. I bought a lot of rat poison, but they would only eat one kind, and I bought and fed them fifty packages at .55 cents apiece. They finally got filled up and we never saw any more of the rascals. We had so many animals visiting us because they were adding to the golf course behind the house, and we were the only residents in that area at that time. Now it's built up all around that area. We had many rattlesnakes around also as large as six feet, two inches long. One day, while watering shrubs in the backyard, a rattler four and a half feet long was following along after me. I guess it thought the hose was another snake. I shot it because a family had just moved in across the road who had a little girl who could have been bitten.

I had a bird feeder and spent many an hour watching the action and habits of different birds. The jays were the wasteful ones that scattered the feed all around on the ground, but the quail would clean it up, so it wasn't really wasted. I found that chick feed was a lot cheaper than bird feed and the birds seemed to like it, so I bought it in large quantities and made fewer trips to the feed mill.

I was driving home from town one day with my sister Ilene and Ruth Mathews and saw what I thought was an awful large dog or a big calf crossing the road quite a distance ahead of us. But when we got up close to it, we saw the largest razorback boar that I have ever seen. It had tusks that looked to be three inches long, and it looked to be over two feet tall. Another unusual animal to see in the wild is the Florida panther, which we saw once while fishing at Arbuckle Creek and we saw it twice in back of our house.

As life was starting to catch up with me, I started having a lot of soreness in my shoulders and neck, partly from age and from an old neck injury. That just took the enjoyment out of playing golf, and being alone most of the summer, I guess I just got tired of living alone away from most of the people I really cared about. So I decided to sell out and move. So that's what got me to Lantana and Boynton Beach. I guess I'm just an old Gypsy!

I rented a room from Grace Mumma and continued to help her get her house ready to sell and tried to be of some help to Floyd when he needed it. I continued running back and forth at least once a week, a 115-mile trip each way. I would stay at Spring Lake a day or two, then head back to Lantana until I sold out in 1998.

It was quite different from my life at Spring Lake. I was sort of lost in a home where I was not the taxpayer although that has the advantage of not paying taxes. But it also takes away a lot of one's freedom and gave me a peon feeling that I guess that I'll have the rest of my life. The problem is, I think I worked too hard for a home that I owned free of debt, then when the so-called golden years came along, I was fool enough to leave my lifelong dream. Well, I feel very fortunate to have friends and a family that are so willing to take me into their homes and treat me very well after doing that dumb thing. I hope that none of my kids follow in my footsteps.

The work at Grace's place was interesting. There were so many things that needed repaired or replaced after years of neglect and wear. I spent a lot of time pulling roots that ran all over the backyard and trimming trees and shrubs. A brick-walled planter ran halfway across the front of the house, and it had a maple tree about eight and a half inches in diameter growing out of it that had pushed the wall over. The roots were starting to heave the house wall. I worked about a week on that to get the stump and roots out. Grace's son, Ronnie, helped me with it one day. And there was a termite problem inside in the woodwork in several places that took many hours to tear out and replace and paint. I think the first job was an access hole in the garage that had been busted out and was an invitation to all kinds of critters. Some very unwelcome rascals, raccoons, squirrels, bees, bugs, etc., took advantage of it. I also rewired the lights in the garage and on the patio. I also dug up and installed all the back and side yard sprinkler system heads. They stuck up out of the ground and were in the way when mowing. I never could understand why they were installed that way. I trimmed the driveway hedge and planted sod on a lot of bare places in the yard. Also, the last couple of years while living at Grace's on High Ridge Road in Lantana, I helped Floyd with Ciara.

Grace sold the place on High Ridge Road and was waiting on the closing when she went to Vermont to visit with her family. She asked me to look for a place in a mobile home park that would answer her needs and wouldn't take as much care as the place she had.

I thought she'd like to be fairly close to her old neighborhood. I had gotten fed up with having a mobile on a rented lot like I had in Whispering Pines. I went to Tropical Breezes where it is all owned by individuals and only one lot to an individual. They were county roads and governed by the owners with one vote to each owner. So there was no outside interests. There was a yearly maintenance, water, and sewer fee set by popular vote. There were three for sale. I narrowed it down to two, and Grace chose one and bought it. It is about a block from Floyd's place, which makes it handy for both of them and me also. There were quite a few things that needed attention. I made arrangements with Grace to rent the back bedroom for my labor and a monthly cash fee.

Well, I started in by taking the metal bifold doors off the closet and making storage shelves in the laundry and replaced them with vinyl folding closet. Grace had a lot of boards that we brought from the other place, plus lumber that I got from the wheelchair ramp that I had built for Floyd when Clara was not able to walk. I made more shelves, a workbench, and tool racks for lawn and garden tools. In other words, I spent a lot of time doing things I enjoyed. And Grace spent a lot of her time doing what she has done most of her life, taking care of and helping older ladies, which, I think, is very commendable.

Floyd and Grace were very good to me as I had several spells of blood pressure and other things that put me in the hospital. They stuck by many hours for which I am very thankful.

I was getting ready to leave Floyd's house one day and had the door of the car open ready to step in, and the next thing I knew, I was flat on my back on the concrete drive. When I picked myself up with Floyd's help, I was dizzy and had a hard time walking, but I got in the car and drove back to the house and sat still for the rest of the day. I was getting around but staggering some for a couple of months after that crack on the bead. So I decided to quit driving a car and made up my mind to sell my Ford. I was at Betty's and she said the lady who cleans for her was looking for a used car that was reliable and in good shape, so she took it out and drove it and liked it, so I sold it to her. She is a mighty fine lady, and I'm glad she got it because it was one of my most liked possessions. Even so, I've had cars for seventy-four years, and I sure don't like not being able to get in my old tin lizzie and driving!

After my last round in the hospital, I decided I would take Betty's advice and make my final move to her and Jack's place. And that's where I am now.

Ilene, Floyd, Mom (Pearl),
Grandma Kennedy, 1927

Floyd, 1940

Burt's 1921 Model T, Arch and Pup

Archer and Burt, 1941

Archer and Burt, 1912?

Floyd and Clara, 1934

Some Anecdotes

T HESE ARE SOME DIFFERENT things that come to mind but not necessarily in the order that they happened. Some funny, some sad, some just…

In the year 1916, I had my first school experience in a little old one-room school. It was supervised by a lady teacher who ran the whole show with an average of around eighteen students, just plain farm kids with the toes of their shoes stubbed out or barefooted in warm weather. In the spring or fall, the classes might be down to ten or twelve as some of the older kids had to stay home and help with farm crops at the harvest seasons. The oldest boy was the janitor and general maintenance man (unless one of the neighborhood *rooster* was trying to get dose to the pretty young teacher).

I think there were only four of us first graders that year, and as always seemed true in all groups of kids, we looked up to the elder teenagers for advice and instructions, which were given at times with evil intent. Well, it was a nice day, so Teach sent us outside to play for our first recess. There was a little storage or coal shed about one by twelve by eight feet high. We chose up sides and us little brats were put on either side of the shed. One of the older kids would take a chunk of coal about three inches around and toss it up off the roof so that it hit the other side and would roll down off the root. The kids on that side would catch it before it hit the ground and then toss it to the other side the same way. Well, about the third toss, one of the older kids fumbled, and of course, I was under that fumble and got that coal right in the middle of my head. It cut a slit about two inches long, and I bled like a stuck hog. I had to quit and the teacher patched me up real nice.

That was the last of my career as an Antony over player! We moved to Warren the next month, and I was glad about that because my brother didn't get to call me a sissy for being a quitter just on account of a little bump on my head! I do not know how old that little schoolhouse was in 1916, but to my knowledge, it still sits at the same location on Arlington Road east of the turnpike overpass in Newton Township.

When we lived on the Wood farm the first time, I was about five years old. Burt was eight, and we had little chores to do like watering the plants. Burt, of course, being eight, was doing some of the hoeing and cultivating. One day, he was cultivating the sweet corn when Mom told me to call him for lunch. I ran out and started up a row of corn and yelled at him. He said he was coming up this row, so we met in the middle of the same row. He was running with the cultivator teeth up and the corn was just high enough, so neither of us could see ahead. So we met with one of those teeth sticking in my leg above my knee. Well, old Doc Meilly came out and stuck a tongue depressor wrapped with gauze dipped in a gallon jug of turpentine and swabbed it out with me screaming, Burt crying, Mom wringing her hands, and that darned old doc grinning. I still have the scar today.

It seems like calling kids for lunch was a bad thing to do at the Wood farm because, about five years later, I was chopping old wood fence pickets into pieces for the stove so Mom could bake bread. Floyd came out to tell me lunch was ready. I had two more to cut, and Floyd got real impatient with me and stuck his barefoot on top of the piece I was chopping at the time the axe was in midair. Well, that was the wrong thing to do as he wound up with five toes almost cut off. Old Doc Fiester came out from Newton Falls and had a real hard time sewing it back together as he was old and shaky and Floyd was kicking. Doc even pulled a couple of stitches out before he could get them secured. Grandma Kennedy was there and the only one in the five of us that wasn't praying for old Doc to get that ordeal over with. Well, Floyd lived through it in spite of not having any anesthetic. He is eighty-six years old now with ten toes and is doing quite well.

While we lived at the I. B. Wood farm about 1919, the Yeager six boys were our close neighbors, and we seldom missed a day that Burt and I didn't work or play with them. We never had a real baseball. We either used a hard rubber ball with a rag wrapped around it, then covered with friction tape. But we played quadruple ball in our minds anyway using dried cow patties for bases. The ground in the pasture was pretty uneven, but the sheep did a great job of keeping the grass mowed short, so we seldom lost a ball. We could make a ball last all summer by retaping it every day or so. We didn't play sides as there were not over six of us big enough to play. The four older kids got three strikes and out, but the two least ones got four strikes. Sometimes, we would lose count and give them five or six strikes just so they wouldn't get mad and quit.

One day, after an hour or so of baseball, we decided to pick a few of the good Monterey cherries that were just waiting for boys to pick and eat before those blue jays and robins got them. There were six trees growing along a fence where several of Mr. Wood's beehives were. Well, each one of us climbed separate trees to avoid an argument, which worked out well until little Johnny (the least of us kids) had to pee. So he climbed down and no sooner got a stream on its way when one of those ornery bees lit on the end of that kid's little dink and stung it. Well, I never heard such a loud scream as he let out, but I sure didn't blame him when we found out what had happened. That was a lesson for the rest of us boys: "Never let a *bee* see you *pee*."

Them Yeager kids were all good boys, hard workers, and honest too. Their father died when the oldest was fourteen and the youngest about three months. But those kids were tough as iron, and along with just a wee bit of help from Burt and me, plus a few days' help from an uncle and a neighbor man, they kept that big 175-acre farm going rather good with a good mother leading them. They raised Durham cattle and two teams of horses and one hundred chickens, several pigs, geese, ducks, and a few guinea hens that acted as sentinels if fox, weasels, or anything else disturbed or invaded the property. Guinea hens are one of the most alert things both night and day, even more so than dogs.

We spent a couple warm sunny Sunday afternoons exploring in the woods, hunting Indian turnips and wild game holes and dens. We sliced and dried the turnips for favors for kids who were mean to us and thought they were smarter than us dumb farmer brats. Those little turnip slices were one of the hottest things that grow.

We played another game that we called sticky ball. We took a short stick and leaned it against another so it set at a forty-five-degree angle, then hit the high side and flipped it up and swung at it with a club like a bat. We would see who could get the highest and the most distance. In those days, our play equipment wasn't fancy and didn't cost a lot, but we had fun and didn't realize that we were poor kids!

I was ten years old when we moved to Parkman Road (or Route 422 in 1920). We were just three lots north of Warren City limits, and at that time, the road was just plain dirt but from the city limits to Summit Street and on to Market Street, it was cinders. Summit and Market Streets were brick and had streetcar tracks on both.

I met some lifelong buddies there, but they are all gone now. Charles (Ducky) Walton was one I spent the most time with as he and I both loved sports, and baseball was our favorite. Both our families had chickens. Ducky lived about a block from us inside the city limits, but in those days, it as legal as long as they were not a nuisance. So Ducky and I both were family heirs to the job of feeding, watering, and cleaning the henhouses before we had permission to play. We sure took advantage of our free time (which was most of the time until our nine o'clock curfew) and most of that time was playing baseball when the weather permitted it.

We both had bicycles and would ride to either Packard Park or Perkins Park. Each had baseball diamonds, and there was always an afternoon or evening game at one of them. There were about six or seven churches that had a league in the city at that time. At most of the game times, the teams had one or two players who were either late or weren't able to play for one reason or another. So either Ducky or I got an invitation to play with them. Of course, they were older than us, but we would fill in at the spots wherever they placed us, which was usually the places where none of them cared to play. We were usually in the outfield or catching. And sometimes we were able to show them us boys were just as good as they were. Of course, we always played our best and we had more practice than they did as we played every day.

To tell of all the wonderful times Ducky Walton and I had in those years would take longer than I may have, so I'll just say we played basketball, soccer, and boxing, but baseball was our game.

Another friend that I had in that era was Jake Schwartz whom I was close to for many years up until I married Alice. Although we were always friends, we just didn't get together as much after I was married. Jake had a new 1928 Ford Roadster, and he liked to drive it wherever the two of us went. But when we dated Alice and Elizabeth, we always drove either my Chevy or his folks' Overland touring car. The four of us went together for a couple of years. Well, like life is, we just drifted apart after a while and didn't see much of one another often.

A couple of my old friends from school days were Bob Maxwell and Lee St. Clair. Bob went on to become a high-up officer in the Salvation Army and Lee got a foreman's job at Taylor Winfield Manufacturing in Warren. Ducky Walton retired from the Warren Police Department and later moved to Florida. I tried several times to locate him in later years but was never able to. I guess I just had too many things to take my mind away from searching and now it's too late.

This is about my basketball career at Lordstown High School. We lived about four miles from the school, and on nights that we played other schools, I had no way of getting back and forth from school to home and back in time to play whether we played at home or away. So I stayed at the school or went across the road to a little store run by the Montgomery family. Norman, or Cy, as he was also called, was on the team and was the center.

On this particular night, we played Gustavus School, and it was a real cold night, so I stayed in the store until time to leave. While waiting, Cy came over and asked me if I would like a glass of fresh cider. I was real thirsty, so I said I sure would. We went next door to his house, and Cy got an old Ford axle and poked it through the ice that was on the top and siphoned us a couple of large glasses of that good sweet cider. It sure did taste good, so I took the second glass that I was offered, but Cy had to go in for his supper so he didn't drink anymore. We drove to Gustavus in Cy's dad's Model T Ford. It was a 1925 touring car, and it was up-to-date with side curtains but no heater as they were extra at that time. So it was a bit cool in zero weather, which it was close to that evening.

So I had no other feelings on the ride that night, except being cold. When we got on the basketball floor, I felt real good for a few minutes while was getting warmed up. But then, all at once, I felt as though the floor was tipping from side to side and I was either running uphill or downhill and then sideways. I was really having a hard time just keeping on the floor right side up. I wound up under our end of the floor when the ball landed in my hands and I made a loop shot and we had the first score. It was real soon after that the very same thing happened, but it turned out that I was at the wrong end of the floor. Well, the coach called time and said to me, "You're not well, are you?" And I really felt okay, but that damned floor just would not cooperate with me. Well, as you can guess, I never got to hear the last of that episode. Anyway, it was a first. One player making the first point for both teams!

When Alice and I were married, we lived with my family that first year at the corner Lyntz Road and Warren Road. We started our little house that year, and Betty was born that same year. I made arrangements with Warren Trimbath to purchase an acre and half of land from him, plus a small amount of money to help on the house construction materials. At his suggestion, he held a mortgage for the place for less than $1,000 at 6 percent interest. I paid $20 a month, plus interest, as long as I could, which was just a little better than a year, then the old stock market went to the bottom and everything came to a standstill and the banks froze all accounts and nobody could get a check cashed. Money got so tight that it just disappeared until President Roosevelt declared a bank holiday until the banks could get straightened out, and of course, that was a real big problem as we had an overinflated economy and people either had mortgages or notes hanging on their shoulders.

The banks had overextended loans, and after a while, they did pay out an allowance of 10 percent to those who had savings, but most people were in debt. The building trade was the first to get hit, and the vultures closed in on us and tore at our lives. So after two and a half years of that, we lost our little home. During that time, Bob was born. After three years of hard work, all Alice and I realized was $310. But we still had our two kids, which was better than all other possessions that anyone can have.

As I see it, World War I was the start in the change in the ways of the people of this country. Thinking back, there is no doubt that some things were made easier, but I don't think people are as happy because there is so much pressure on people today. We had more freedom then, and I don't think we had so many clowns and crooks in Washington running our lives. Then we had a few statesmen running things! Of course, that's only my opinion!

Enough complaining! I believe there are better things to talk about, such as kids' cute actions. I've always liked the little innocent things kids said and did a lot more than the actions and stupid things grown-ups do and say.

Revenge Is Sweet

WHEN BETTY WAS VERY young, we had a little Boston terrier that she would carry around and hug like a doll, but I guess Bob was a bit rougher with the pup, and one day, I came in the house and heard a big commotion in the front room. When I rushed in, I saw Bob on the couch with the pup, and it was yipping and Bob was squalling. When I asked Bob what the problem was, he said, "He bit my hand, so I bit his tail."

TO BE (A KID) OR NOT TO BE (A CAT)

When Archer was about four and Jack was two, we had an old calico cat that was the kids' pet. She had kittens, and they were fed in a tin plate in the backyard. One day, Fanny called to me that I should look to see what those boys were doing. Well, I looked out and that pie pan had a boy on each side of it, licking up that bread and milk just like a couple of kittens. I thought that was cute thing for them to do, but Fanny, like all moms, had to make them leave the cat's dish to the cats. She reminded them that they were kids and not kittens. I decided that Fanny was right in a harsh, but wise, way.

SISTER DEAREST

Kay Ellen was about three years old when she adopted Jimmy, our youngest, and really mothered him until he was drafted into the military. She took extra good care of him. Fact is, if he was too quiet, she would pinch or bite him to make him cry so she could have a reason to coddle him and tell him how she loved him and felt sorry for him. She dressed, fed, and cared for him like a good mom, even tied his shoes until he was drafted. Then he sat on the stairs about an hour every day for a week while she taught him how to tie his shoes. He said later that he just looped instead of tied and stuffed the strings in the top of his boots or shoes.

Friends Forever

One day, I was in the kitchen talking to Fanny and we heard dogs barking out by the road, so we went to the front window to see what was causing them to make such a fuss. There was a man sitting straddle on top of our mailbox, and our dogs were standing near and barking at him. Queenie was a real friendly dog and always greeted everybody with a friendly yip and a wagging tail. Well, she was just greeting that man and Mutt was just a half-grown pup. Mutt was joining in the barking and playfully nipping at Queenie's back legs. It was a funny sight seeing a grown man sitting on a mailbox. We finally recognized the man on the mailbox as Lee Beveridge who lived down the road.

Well, when Queenie saw that he wasn't going to get down off his seat and play with her, she turned and trotted away with Mutt still nipping at her heels and barking away. I went out and helped Lee off the mailbox, and he told me that he had run out of gas down the road and was walking to our place to get a can of gas when Queenie attacked him. He said he jumped on the mailbox to get away from her and Mutt saved his life by chasing her off. He said that Mutt was the greatest dog in the world. He didn't realize that Mutt just wanted to play with Queenie and show off. Queenie was later killed on the road by a speeder. Mutt later became a frequent visitor at the Beveridge household, even spending the night at times. He also kept Lee company at his car sales office when business was slow.

More Dog Stories

We had another little dog when the kids were small. He was a fox terrier named Spot. He was a real fireman! He hated fire and would jump on and stomp out a cigarette butt or burning paper.

Another thing he didn't like was men who wore hard-billed caps like policemen and mailmen wore. He would just go crazy and bite at them. He also couldn't stand slapping at one another when we were playing. He was also killed on the road by a speeder.

Fanny had quite an experience with a neighbor's boxer. There was a plowed field between our houses, and one day, when I came home from work, I saw Fanny standing in our driveway. That boxer was in the field, and they were just looking at each other, and I could see that Fanny was awfully angry. And that damned dog looked like he was smiling, and you can be sure that Fanny wasn't liking that! Well, that boxer had just killed three little ducks that Fanny had gotten for the kids at Easter time. She was throwing clods of dirt at him but just couldn't throw far enough to hit him. Each time she threw, he was just a foot too far from her, and each step she took forward, he took one back. The dog survived, but not through any help from Fanny. We were all happy when Mays moved and took their dog with them.

Interesting Carpentry

This is just one of the things I often recall when I think of the different things I got into while working at carpentry. We had a call from a lady named Helen Hart Hurlbert who owned the *Warren Tribune Newspaper*. Her husband had owned the Bostwick Steel Lathe in Niles Ohio and had passed away from some kind of virus at the Great Lakes Naval Station just a short time before we were contacted about the job.

The original job was to repair all the windows of the house by putting in new cords for the weight-balanced double-hung windows and repair all other parts that were damaged or worn out.

Well, the first day, we started working there about eleven forty-five and a girl of about fifteen or sixteen years old came into the room we were working in and said that she was in a domestic science class in school She said she was learning how to cook and bake and wanted us to taste her cooking and baking and give her our honest opinion of it. Well, she really put us on the spot, but we agreed to do our best. Well, she picked some real good recipes and did a great job with them, so we didn't have to carry a lunch as long as she was more than happy to use us as guinea pigs.

Before we left the job, Mrs. Hurlbert asked me if we would do another job that she really was wanting to do to complete a project her husband had started before he passed away. One project was a wine rack and the other was an *outside* toilet in the basement to be constructed like the old-time outhouses. We had a bit of a problem getting the proper materials such as wide boards all in one piece of good material for the three-holer and the red-white corncobs, as well as the clapboard roof. It was as authentic as possible. We took six-inch blocks of wood and split them to about one-fourth thick for the roof, put a rack on the wall to hold the corncobs, and hung an old Sears catalog beside it. There was a quarter-moon cut in the door, a three-hole seat with lids that had a mirror under each, so when raised up, you were looking at what some people might call you when they get a bit riled up at you. Then she had an artist come and paint some hollyhocks on the outside which really made it look like the best little old backhouse in town. Then she had their company, Bostwick Steel Lathe, make a wine rack that reached from one foot above the floor to the ceiling and nine feet wide. I don't know how many bottles it held, but she had every port filled. That's the story of the last three-holer that I remember having anything to do with.

More Days Gone By

I've had a lot of good friends over the years, but as in all things, there are some that I was a bit closer to and, perhaps, were around a lot more than others, so they come to mind more than others.

George Mathews was one of them. We went fishing together many times locally, and at least once or twice a year, we went to Canada with a group of friends that consisted of mostly couples. Sometimes, there were more men than women. My brother-in-law, John Kean, and I usually shared a cabin by ourselves as Fanny didn't fish and Ilene seldom went along. We did our own cooking and housekeeping chores, except when everyone got together and had fish dinners outside when the weather permitted and inside the big hunting lodge when the weather was bad. We stayed at Drinkwalters Camp in Nippising on the South River. Jerry Drinkwalter and his wife, who ran the fishing and hunting camp, were good people and always friends of the Mathews, and during the years, we visited their camp. George went there more often than I did as he hosted clients of his that were buyers and guests of the Heltzel Steel Co. of Warren. Oh, George was a salesperson and demonstrator for the company. They built and sold concrete forms and road machinery.

On one of our trips to Canada, there were fourteen of us, and Jerry offered to be our guide and cooked a big fish dinner up on one of the rock islands about five miles out in the lake. There were two little scrub oak and maple bunches, one at either end of the island that served as restrooms, women at one end of the island, men at the other. Jerry wasn't feeling very well that day and asked a couple of the fellows if they would help get things ready for the cooking of the fish. One of them said he would start the fire. Well, there were two piles of driftwood and branches and twigs off the trees that Jerry piled up in the off-season so things would be handy when he was busy. And he had two little grills about fourteen inches high with folding legs that he would put two large iron skillets on. He put a pound of butter in one and a pound of bacon in the other to fry the fish in.

Well, the fire builder just threw a match into one of the piles of brush, and the other eager beaver tossed a half-gallon can of Heinz baked beans into it when the fire got going good, and when poor old Jerry came back, I think he got a lot sicker. One of his fuel sources was destroyed and the can of beans exploded, and there were beans scattered all over a radius of a quarter acre. Joe Mathews, George, and I were out of sight at the shoreline filleting and getting the fish ready to fry, so we missed all the commotion until we heard the bean explosion.

Well, you can be sure we never asked those two guys to do any chores again. Poor Jerry died of cancer late that same fall and couldn't be buried until the ground thawed out the next summer. We sorely lost a good friend. Ruth Mathews still keeps in touch with Jerry's wife. George is gone now, but Ruth and I still keep writing each other at least a couple times a month. Joe's wife is still living, but in an assisted-living home, but all the rest are gone now.

Aubrey and Mary Totten were another couple of good friends. Aubrey and Mary went along with the group one year, but Mary didn't care to fish but did go out with the gang a couple days for companionship. She spent the rest of the days cleaning all our cabins cleaner than they were used to and fixing meals instead of taking it easy, but that was Mary's way. Aubrey is in a rest home now with multiple problems of old age. Mary is living in their beautiful home that I built for them in 1957 on Route 305 in Cortland.

Ernest Helmich was another good friend. Ernie was born in Alaska in about 1902, the son of a German missionary. Old Ernie was a good businessman whose virtue was honesty, and he expected others to be likewise, so much so that he seemed to be tightfisted at times. I remember one time while fishing in Canada I was in the front of my boat and Ernie was in the rear. We were trolling through a channel into a cove where we usually caught at least a strike of some sort when the boat gave an awful jolt and rocked back and forth. I turned around to see what was happening and asked Ernie if he had hooked onto a big one.

I saw him standing up in the boat (all six feet four of him) chattering to himself. He said to me, "That damned Englishman at the store beat me out of three cents in the money exchange this morning." That was Ernie's way, but when we went places together, he always insisted on paying for everything as I did the driving in my car. Ernie and I were partners in a business deal, and every Sunday morning at seven fifteen, he would knock on our door and he would be standing there, ready for a stroll out through the woods and pastures. We observed nature and picked wild asparagus, berries, hickory nuts, or anything that was in season. We even hunted rabbits in winter. There were always many birds to be seen—woodcock, hawks, owls, wood ducks, and others; also, deer were a common sight.

One day, while we were coming back to the house, Ernie was telling me that he had dug up a couple hills of his potatoes and how nice they were, some of them the size of a fist and larger. When we were passing my garden, he asked if I had dug any of mine and I said no, so I pulled up a dead vine and we were both surprised as there was one of the biggest potatoes we had ever seen, along with two more that were larger than the ones Ernie had. His eyes got big, and I could see that he was not happy. He said, "What the hell did you do to make them grow that big?" I told him I just put a bunch of leaves in the trenches and scattered a little fertilizer in and dropped the taters in and covered them, then hoed and cultivated them same as I always did.

Well, Ernie didn't believe me, I guess, because he just left without saying a word and didn't show up for those Sunday-morning strolls for about a month. Then one Sunday morning, I was in the garage where I had fourteen bushels of potatoes sitting along the wall in baskets, and Ernie walked in right past me with a bag and a basket in his band. Then without a word, he set the bag on the workbench and turned around and picked six nice potatoes up and put them in his basket and put it in his car. He hesitated a minute, then came back in and said, "Even trade. See you later" and left. Well, I looked in the bag and found twenty beautiful gladiola bulbs worth a lot more than the spuds he'd taken. That was my honest friend Ernie, a great guy!

By the way, that potato weighed two and one-fourth pounds.

A Bit of History of Woodworking

I CAN'T REMEMBER MY GREAT-GRANDFATHER'S first name right now, but it is on his gravestone in the Orangeville cemetery. At my age, it's hard to find folks to help me with these olden times subjects, so I just have to go with the way I remember it. The first of the Joneses that I know of was a Cooper, or barrel maker, in the early eighteen hundreds. Then there was Grandpa Jones who worked hewing logs and timbers of many shapes and sizes; he also built cabins, barns, and bridges. My dad hauled logs to the Calender sawmill on north Elm Street in Warren close to Carter lumber near the bypass. Then the next generation was my brother Burt and myself. We worked together at carpentry for many years building anything made of wood, from fine homes to the old-fashioned three-holers.

Burt's specialty was hanging doors and finishing, mine was stairs, cabinets, and framing. But we both did whatever job needed to be done. We had both cut a lot of trees with crosscut saws and buzzed a lot of firewood for winters. I had a team of horses and cut and hauled the last of the chestnut trees in our area to Skinny Kings sawmill where he sawed them into timbers and sold them for the timbers in the Quimby shelter house in Warren near West Junior School. The chestnut trees had a killing blight a couple years, and all those wonderful trees in the state of Ohio died. At least I've never seen one since then.

All my boys have worked some carpentry work at one time or another, either part- or full-time. Archer and Jack have worked almost all their lives at it full-time. They are both fine carpenters who both

103

worked with me some. Archer contracted after I retired, and Jack worked with Mellott of Cortland and Archer gave up the headaches of self-employment and went to work for Warren Engineering where he retired from in 2000. Jack has a shop of his own and does some specialty woodwork and does layout work for Mellott and works some with his son, Jack Jr., who worked with his dad with Mellott for a couple of years. Jim has also done some freelance carpentry. Archer's son, Martin, also works carpentry for Warren Engineering. So that makes six generations of woodworkers. They have reputations for doing fine work, which makes this old man proud of them. Bob worked with me at times also. He was an electrical engineer at Packard Electric, and Jim is a traffic dispatcher at LTV Steel, both good at their jobs, and that adds to my pride in my boys.

Now for the girls. I adopted Phyllis when she was six years old. She has been a very faithful daughter. In all these years, she has always remembered me on my birthday and Father's Day and has been very thoughtful to me and thought of by me the same as the other girls. She has worked many different jobs all her life since she graduated from Lordstown High School—elevator operator, printshop worker, and retail sales. She is married and seems to be living a pleasant life with her husband, Carl Juillerat. I am happy to call her my daughter.

Next is Betty, who is a very talented girl who graduated from Newton Falls High School. She went to work for Gold Tone Photography Studio in Warren, became manager there, then managed a Gold Tone Studio in Columbus where she met and married John (Jack) Huling who was in the Air Force. He served in the British Isles, then went to dental school and later opened an office in Miami where Betty managed the office. She also managed an office for a doctor in the same complex. She is now being a damn good cook for Jack and me.

Frances (Fanny) Dale was born December 19, 1942. Santa Claus was a bit early that year, so Mom and I got our present early. Frances graduated from Lordstown where she participated in all the athletics and later managed a ladies' softball team and also helped coach boys' little league. She drove school bus, worked at Thomas Steel, then worked at Specialty Pipe & Tube where she met and married Steve Chermansky. She is a fine seamstress. She now works for Lordstown schools as substitute secretary and as an assistant to the career education coordinator, a very talented girl.

Kay Ellen is a graduate of Lordstown schools. She was our smallest kid in stature, but not the least in any other way. Of course, the baby girl was a homegirl and helped her mom and dad a lot. She is an excellent housekeeper and wife to her husband, Bruce Ballentine. I know she is because he told me she was and is yet. They work together real well at yard work and restoring custom cars. She probably knows more about cars than most men. She also turns out beautiful writing cards on her computer. She babysat for Archie and Connie when their kids were small and Connie worked at the bank. Her work outside the home was a few years as democratic committee woman for the election board.

So you can see why I am so proud to have those eight wonderful kids and four good sons-in-law and four great-daughters-in-law. And all the sons and sons-in-law served with honor in the military.

I could go on praising my kids and their mothers forever and not be able to do them justice. I only hope that I have not slighted any of them or told anything that will hurt anyone. I love them all equally!

My version of what I saw on TV on September 11, 2001. A very sad day for America! Shortly after 8:45 a.m., the news on TV announced that the World Trade Center in New York City had been hit from the air by either a plane or bomb. The upper part of that 110-story tower was burning. It showed great clouds of black smoke rolling from it, and shortly after, a big passenger plane rammed into the other tower. It was ablaze, then what seemed like seconds later, it just seemed to crumble from inside straight down to the ground. Being in construction most of my life and several years as a fireman, I had never seen a building disintegrate like that steel and masonry building did. Then just minutes later, the other twin tower went down the same way. Then just a few minutes later, the word came that the Pentagon building was also hit. A hell of a day!

There has been a lot of change in the country in the last seventy years. Back in those days, a lot of the country was quite a good deal of wilderness, and many of the roads that are paved now were just a wagon track through the wooded areas between farms and just slag roads between villages and towns. It was 1925 before Lordstown to Warren Route 45 was improved with limestone slag. Until about 1945, there was a road that is at the extreme south side of Lordstown Township that I think is now called Gladstone Road that was a wagon track with grass and weeds growing in between the tire tracks. From Route 45 to the west was a little stony hill that the folks around there called Ghost Bill. It was called that because in those early days, with just a very few autos in the country once in a while at night, the car lights would show a flash of light as they turned a corner from over in the Milton Lake area about four miles away.

As there was only a couple of times a week, this would happen. Most people who saw it really thought it was a spook of some sort. Of course, in those days, folks didn't have a lot of entertainment since it was before TV, so it was a popular situation for people to spend an evening discussing ghosts and other topics such as the moon and the stars. But after General Motors built that Chevy plant in Lordstown, things have changed and spoiled a perfect place for young folks to spend enjoyable evenings. There is a paved road there now, and some smart kids figured out where the ghosts came from and also about the birds and the bees.

Now days there ain't much of anything for the young folks to wonder about. Well, anyway, about seventy years later, there are several nice homes on that road. My son, Archer, built two of them for GM employees. And the old log cabin that an old character named Warren Goff used to live in is long gone. Charley Sheldon and I used to hunt raccoon and anything else those old dogs of ours would chase up in that area. We were surprised many times at the strange animals those old dogs scared up. A few times, when we were expecting a raccoon after a long chase, we found domestic cats that had gone wild. But those days have gone by.

These are some remembrances from the early 1930s. Charlie Sheldon was an old friend and neighbor for many years. We were both poor as church mice and were doing anything to earn enough to exist on. We both had families, and it was an uphill struggle in those times. Dollars were so scarce; everything was figured in cents. We worked for farmers mostly as that was about the only operation that wasn't closed down because people still had to eat. We both worked for a farmer, helping fill silo all day in the rain. Charlie and I loaded a wagon. We were ankle-deep in mud, and the corn was in big bundles and heavy as hell. Well, after ten hours, both of us were awfully tired even though we were both used to hard physical work. We went up to get our pay and told the man we were done. He asked what we thought we should have, and we told him .35 cents an hour. He said that was too much.

Well, he finally said he was short of help, and since we had done the work of three men, he grudgingly paid us. The usual farm wage was about $1.50 for eight and $2.00 for special labor like thrashing or filling silo. We worked quite often for the Stitle twins, Charlie and Emery. Although they were twins, they were very unalike in most ways, but both great guys. I worked for them a lot more than the other young guys did. I guess because Alice baked bread for them, and they liked it and ate a lot of it. Emery was short and fat with sandy hair, and Charlie was slim and about two inches taller with black hair. They got along good but argued sometimes, but only in German if there was anyone but me around. I guess they considered me as a part of their family. They were mainly produce farmers but kept a small dairy, pigs, and chickens for their own use and two teams of horses, a Ford tractor, a Ford truck, a 1924 model T, and a 1934 model A in later years. They butchered three thirty-pound pigs every fall and bought a quarter of beef twice a year for home use as they most always had one or two of the help for dinner in the busy season.

They were both fine cooks and took turns at it. And they always put plenty on the table. They raised potatoes, cabbage, cauliflower, squash, and tomatoes. They raised hay and grains to feed their stock, so it was an all-around operation, and they did a super job of it. They were born and raised in a log cabin which stood on twenty-two acres of land at the back end of the farm they bought before they were twenty years old. They earned the money working for other farmers and raising strawberries with a little loan from another kind farmer. They paid him back in just a couple of years.

They also took care of their parents for a few years before they passed away. I worked for them for a few years during the bad times for $1.50 a day, but on real busy days, I would stay and help with evening chores, and they gave me a quarter extra and my supper. I was one of the last to be a part of their days here on earth. I took Emery to have an infected tooth pulled, and he died a week later with a strep infection from it. Charlie had what they called in those days hardening of the arteries, and I took him on his last trip from home to a hospital. Both were sad times for me.

Sometimes, while writing this, I think I had better go back to school and try to learn how to write, spell, and be a little more literate. But I guess I am a bit late for that, so I guess I'll just have to keep on being what I am.

But there is still time to say that I'm proud of my kids and love them! I think this might be a good time to say what I remember of the Jones family. This is a little history of my ancestors as I remember from years as a kid and growing to almost maturity. Some of this I witnessed and the rest I heard from my elders. I have no other proof except Grandpa's talks to me when he lived with us.

My great-grandfather Jones was from Connecticut and had his own copper business moving to Shakleyville Pennsylvania where my grandpa Jones was born in 1858. He married my grandmother Emma Spitler, and they had three sons and one daughter. Their names were Harry, Arthur, Edna, and Carl. Grandpa was of Scottish and Irish descent. Grandma was three-fourths American Indian. My great-grandfather Spitler was three-fourths Dutch and one-fourth American Indian, and my great-grandmother was full-blooded Indian. Both of the families were from the area near the Shenango Valley in Pennsylvania.

Grandpa Jones was self-employed most of his life. He was a farmer and had a livery stable on Park Avenue in Warren across from the courthouse, furnishing horses and carriages for the surrounding area. He had four brothers that I know of although my history of that side of the family is not clear enough in my mind to try to dwell on it. I do remember the brothers were Grandpa Columbus Anderson (Lum), Franklin (Frank), Newton (Newt), and Washington (Wash).

The four brothers decided in the late 1870s or '80s to homestead in Kansas somewhere in the Topeka area. Well, it must have been a long slow trip. Granddad said in those days roads were just wagon tracks through the country and there were very few bridges. They used mules and horses for power and the old schooner or Conestoga wagon for hauling and living quarters while traveling.

Twenty-five miles was an exceptional good day's travel. They took some food staples like flour, salt, coffee, and smoked and salted meats as towns were far between then and money was scarce. They also had to take seeds for crops, so they were loaded to the limit. And after all the hardships they went through to get their new land, they had three straight years of hot winds and dry weather. Three of the families were broke and discouraged and went back to their old home areas in Ohio and Pennsylvania. Frank went to farming, Newt became a grocer in Meadeville, and Grandpa Lum to farming. Newt stayed in Kansas and, after a struggle for several years, became a successful wheat farmer.

Later, Grandpa and Grandma went their different ways and Grandpa came to stay at our place in the teens. He went to work at the Boardman Machine shop and later to Beaver Pipe & Tool Company near where the Packard Electric is now on Dana Avenue. Until 1922, they paid any amount in the $10 to $20 bracket in gold. Grandpa used to be proud to show me his gold coins that he saved to later buy a model T Ford and four lots in back of our place on Parkman Road. The lots were between Maxwell Avenue and Niblock Avenue. It was the sports field for all the kids in the neighborhood as long as we lived on Parkman Road. We lived there from 1910 until 1924, the longest time my folks lived in any one place.

I wish I had talked more to my grandpa Jones about our ancestors, but in those years, at my ages from ten to fifteen years, I wasn't much interested in the history of my ancestors as I should have been. Also in those days, mixed marriages were frowned on so some of the white folks didn't tell if they had Indian or African or any of the colored bloods in their veins. I'm just not sure what Adam and Eve's color was, and I guess it doesn't matter. That is all I can remember on that subject at this time.

I believe that nature is the place to go for truth or as near to it as you can get. Of course, there are a few critters that I just don't care much for. Two of them are rats and mice. Now some folks don't like snakes and fire ants, but I've found if you leave them alone and don't disturb them, they won't bother you. Except the ants, they do sort of become quite a nuisance, but they are not so sneaky about it. I prefer dogs and horses as my number one pick. I guess because I have had some very close friends of both. Of course, I like almost all of nature's offsprings.

I want to say a few things about this typewriter I bought. I just can't understand why salespeople tell such big whoppers just to sell an uneducated folks a product. It must be that they have a surplus of one thing and just try to get rid of it! That young fella that sold me this machine said that I ought to get about four writing tapes and one roll of eraser tape. Well, that jasper either didn't understand this contrary machine or else he just told an outright whopper 'cause this damn thing eats up two rolls of eraser tape to one roll of the other, and that's a fact!

I think I must be the most, or next to the most, confused guy in the world 'cause most everyone else just seems to be able to go along every day and take things just the way they are, but old me just can't seem to keep in line with the way things are. I just wonder about the darndest things. Some folks say I worry about things that can't be changed, but that shoots the Darwin theory all to hell, doesn't it? I just guess that I am just a nosy old fart. I wonder about a lot of things that seem strange to me, like when I was going to school. I wondered why, if the teachers knew so darned much, then why did they have to ask the questions and the kids were supposed to come up with the answers? It sure did take me a long time to get the answer to that through my head. By that time, it was most too late for me to see how dumb I was.

Another of my problems is that it took me so long to learn the main reason for going to school. I thought school was just one of the things a kid had to go through to grow of age. But in later years, I came to realize that the three Rs were very necessary. Anyhow, I sure am sorry that I took the wrong approach to learning, and I must have been a pain in the neck (or elsewhere) to some of my teachers. I remember one time a music teacher tried to make Ducky Walton and I sing a duet because neither of us liked to sing or be in any part of the music business, except where no one could observe or hear us. We pretended we had sore throats, but I guess we didn't fool that old girl because she kept right on our butts till she finally wore us down to a frazzle.

And so we were embarrassed in front of all those kids in our class. I looked at Ducky, and I thought if I looked as sickly as he did, we had better give it a whirl, so I elbowed him in the ribs. We gave it the best we had, but I guess it wasn't good enough for that old girl 'cause she threw up her hands and put her food down hard enough to make the floor tremble on that stage. Ducky and I were singing what we thought was good, but before we got over six words of our song out, she said we sounded like a couple of donkeys braying. Needless to say, we got poor grades on our next report cards. I guess you could say that I just wasn't born with a voice for singing, and it hasn't improved.

I never was a dancer although all my immediate family was excellent at that art. I did step on the dance floor at Kelly (Archer and Connie's daughter) and John's wedding reception with my great-granddaughter Chrissy (Fanny's granddaughter, DeeAnn's daughter) and did okay. Her escort was a young boy who wasn't thrilled about girls yet.

Cutting the rug with Chrissy

These are a few things that I remember of the olden days in the early 1900s. We didn't have as many gadgets to entertain us in those days, especially on the farms. About the handiest thing was the old wall hung crank telephone that was mostly party lines of not more than six or eight on a line. They were all given different rings instead of numbers, such as two shorts and a long. Because they were all on the same line, there were no secrets or scandals to be talked about on the phone. We also had phonographs, and the darn things had to be cranked and the records changed after each record. There was none of that relaxing in a big easy chair with a remote to do the getting up for you. Radios were just beginning in the thinking stage. I don't remember of TV being talked about in those early teens. In those days, families, weather, crops, and crop prices with the government were the big issues that were talked about.

On the farms, family, and crops were the main subjects, and I think are very important yet today. One of the simple pleasures we had in the fall was the corn-husking bees. Several of the neighbors and friends would get together and set a date for a day of husking at the farm that had the first mature corn. The men would get bushel baskets ready for each person, men and women alike. The girls and boys, all twelve years and older, were included. Usually, the older people who had infirmities that would interfere with their ability to participate in the husking would tend to the household chores and take care of the younger kids. The kids were pretty much the same then as they are now, only they were taught better manners with a bit harsher discipline. When I was a kid, it was a serious thing to talk back to elders or show disrespect in any way, but the world is changing every day (maybe for the better?). That last bit about raising kids would be better ignored as I don't believe an old fart like me should criticize.

I'll get on with the husking bee. Well, it was, more or less, a contest. First, it was the women that played the important part of the affair. They furnished great meals like we used to have at our picnics. I tell you, there is nothing that can compare to good food cooked on one of those old woodburning stoves. One highlight was finding the first red ear of corn. There was a limited number of red mixed with the yellow and white. The first to red ear would hold it up and yell loud enough for everyone to hear. The first red ear of the day got a choice of a kiss of an eligible person of the opposite sex, the first dance that evening, a pick of the person to eat with, or the first tin of cider.

Of course, it being a social affair, there was always a keg with a little more age on it for some of the grown folks who didn't care for the sweeter stuff. Of course, the men eighteen and older usually picked the one with more age, and now and then, one of the younger males would try to lie about their age by a year or two but most played fair. It was kind of nice to be young and single and find the first red ear because, in that case, you got to kiss the girl of your choice if she was willing, and most times they were mostly good sports. The music was almost always a fiddle or mouth organ. My dad called for a lot of those old square dances.

At the end of the day, the person who husked the most baskets was allowed to brag about it for as long as folks would listen. Then came the eating and dancing with a few drinks along the way. People most always tried to get back home by midnight as farm chores had to start about 5:00 a.m. the next day. Everybody had a good time with very little expense and a farmer got a lot of corn husked and stored for the winter. All were happy, that is unless one of those young folks earned the right to kiss someone else's girl, which might make a sour grape or so. But as always, life goes on. I guess that's the way we humans are.

In the old days, there weren't as many things like TV, radio, or other mechanical devices as there are today for entertainment. We did have movie theaters, but they were silent and black-and-white. We did have a Victrola record player, and later Granddad Jones got a player piano for Mom. It played from rolls, and us young folks had a great time with that thing. We just pumped the hell out of it for several years until radios got popular!

I was ten years old when I can remember hearing a radio for the first time in the home of a friend and neighbor, Lee St. Clair, in 1920. While we lived in the Warren area, we played every athletic sport, even hockey. For a puck we used a snuff can filled with mud to make it heavy and used crooked tree limbs or any stick of wood we could hit the puck with. We played on Parkman Road which is Route 422 as it was about the only smooth surface we had available. It was newly paved with brick, and those days, cars were not used much during weekdays, only for the work transportation. Only the wealthy folks had more than one car in the family, so traffic was not much of a problem. Sometimes we could play on that road for up to a half hour at a time without having to stop for a car to pass.

But one day, we had a tragedy that ended our hockey game forever on that road. A very good buddy of mine misjudged the speed of a new Buick driven by a Cleveland businessman who was either in a hurry or was testing the car for speed. Well, the result was my friend Donald was hit in the back of his head and had a piece of his skull the size of a half dollar knocked out. That was an awfully sad day for all of us who knew Donald Coffer.

I spent most of my time when not in school at my uncle George Kuntz's farm in Paris Township where we played every game that kids played. I always liked the country living although it was a harder way of life in many ways. My uncle was never meant to be farmer. Although he and his sons worked hard at it, they had only mediocre crops. His boys Harold, Glen, and Russell and I did men's work from the time Harold and I were eleven years old. Of course, kids on the farms in those days were expected to do some chores either inside or outside of the house or barn from the age of six years and up, boys and girls alike. At the age of twelve, we were expected to do the same work as grown-ups. It was a good life anyway. We never heard of drugs in those days, only stories of the opium dens where rich folks sometimes got caught going into.

Well, us farm kids never dreamed of going to one of those places; we were thinking of the simpler things in life. The younger kids ran races rolling barrel hoops by patting them along with a stick about a foot long. Then there was that age old game of hide-and-seek that was played from the time we could walk until we got married. Sometimes it could get complicated if someone got riled up if their mate was caught hiding out with a person of the opposite sex. A natural reaction! But us teenagers sorta enjoyed that part of the game. I guess you could call that a natural reaction also.

My two cousins and I got a very enjoyable day about every two weeks. It was a trip to Windham to take grain to the feed mill to be traded for flour and groceries and sometimes a sack or two of ground feed for the livestock. We usually got a nickel ice-cream cone and a ten-cent bag of candy, along with groceries to take home. We had enough candy to share with the family since you got about a pound for a dime. And if the grocery order was big enough, the kind grocer would add a little extra candy.

Additions to the Old Days

WHEN WE LIVED WITH my grandma Jones at the hotel in Newton Falls, there was a little old black man that did menial chores like keeping the water buckets filled and fuel in the boxes by the stoves and just general outside chores. His name was John. He was a good human being and had only one enemy that I knew of, and that was a little poodle that Grandma had. It would snap at John, making him miserable until he gave the pup a snack, which made them friends. John was a very religious fella and went to church every Sunday. Sunday morning, he would put his best suit on with a cord for a belt and a big red flower in his lapel There was a mirror over a vanity that was a two-inch-by-sixteen-by-eight-feet plank that had five tin wash pans, towels, soap, and a bucket of fresh cold water with a long handled dipper hanging on each bucket. John would stand in front of that mirror and tickle himself in the ribs.

Everything in that hotel was modern and kept in top notch condition. The bath was about three hundred feet in the back of the hotel, which was the west bank of the Mahoning River. For the ladies and more modest folks, there was a washtub that John would temper with a bit of warm water for a small fee. Grandma was a great cook, and the old hotel did quite well until the streetcar track was completed in that area. After that, Grandma went to work for some rich folks in Warren. She had offers from many other folks to do cooking only, but she was satisfied where she was and stayed put until she was eighty years old.

I remember my first tooth-pulling experience. My brother Burt was a couple years older than me and, of course, knew almost everything about pulling teeth. I had a tooth that was loose, and Burt told me he knew how to pull it, that it wouldn't hurt a bit. He also said that I couldn't tell Mom or she would pull it and that would hurt. He said I had to close my eyes until he got everything fixed up to pull it. He had me stand over by the kitchen while he looped a string around the tooth and tied the other end to the doorknob. Then he slammed the door shut. Well, that old tooth wasn't quite as loose as I thought it was. So you can bet that was last time Burt ever got a chance to practice his dental expertise on me.

Skipping ahead a few years, I was fourteen years old and visiting at Kuntz's in Paris Township when Mr. Fakler stopped in and wanted to see if my cousin, who was a year older than me and wanted to work for him. Harold wasn't the most ambitious boy, and it didn't take a whole lot of coaxing by his folks to have him stay home and help there. I think he knew what was involved in that job since a neighbor friend of his had the job the previous year. So he asked me if I wanted the job. Well, I got the job and called home to have my brother Burt come get me so I could get some clothes. Two days later, I started to work.

I felt right smart as that job was to pay me two big ones (a dollar was worth a whole lot back in those days) and for being *just a kid helper*. But I soon found out that I had to earn it. In the morning, work started at 5:00 a.m. in the barn, milking three big Holstein cows. Those cows had the biggest teats with the smallest holes for the milk to be squeezed through. It was an awful job to get three of those monsters squeezed out before breakfast. The first morning after that battle with those three old cows faucets, I could hardly lift my cup of coffee; in fact, I think I had to bend my head down to reach the cup.

Then it was time to go to the barn and get the horses curried and harnessed and ready for work. If the man who operated the engine hadn't been there that morning, I might have gotten hurt or killed because he told me about how ornery those horses were. He said the black one would kick and crowed a fella against the stall, and the gray horse would reach around and bite, especially a stranger (which I was). Well, I stood back of that black horse for a minute or so just talking real sweet to him and trying to get up my nerve to go in beside that bugger.

While making up my mind to go in, I saw a wooden stick about an inch and a half in diameter and sixteen inches long. I stepped quick in beside him with that stick crossways next to my belly, and that brute lunged over at me, but he hit that stick with his nose and decided that wasn't quite the right thing to do. I then gave him a whack on the hip with that club to let him know that I wouldn't stand for that crap. We got along real well after that.

The gray mare lived up to her reputation too. When I walked in beside her, she reached around with her teeth in a mean fashion as if she was warning me. Well, I just took the hint and gave her a sock on the nose with that stick that made her cry, or I guess snort as I don't think horses cry, and I never had her try to frighten me again.

Then there was the job of water hauling three times a day. The wagon had a five-hundred-gallon tank, plus a platform on top to stand on with a handle about four and a half feet long and two inches around that I got my exercise pumping that tank full three times a day. And I had to oil and grease about forty fittings on the separator and take care of the horses. The engineer took care of the steam engine, and Frank mostly either just shot the breeze with farmers or searched around to see if he could find any fault with Brownie the engineer or me. I had to go back to school a week late because old Frank asked me to work an extra week because he had a hard time finding another whipping boy!

The thrashing machine was a lot better than the flail that they used in my granddad's day to beat the grain loose from the straw, but the combines came along sometime in the late thirties or early forties, and by the early fifties, the old steam engine and the old grain separator were in the past. *Good old days.*

The grain thrashing has changed so much in the time since I was a kid on that farm but remained somewhat the same until the fifties. The grain cutting was the first step done by a machine called a binder. If the weather was extremely wet or there was a high wind that knocked the grain down, then the cutting was done by hand with a tool called a cradle that was like a scythe, only it had wooden arms that extended up from the heel of the blade and curved the same as the blade. It held the stems until an amount accumulated enough to make a bundle. Then it was tied by using a few of the stems of straw twisted together to make ties. That was the method used until the binder took over.

The binder was a great labor and time-saver which cut, tied the twine, and dropped the bundles where they were put into shocks. This required two to four horses to pull it, one person to drive and one to two people to follow and gather and shock the bundles, then put a couple of spread out bundles for caps to help shed water until dry enough to thrash.

The first thrashing machines were hand-fed by a person standing on a platform on the rear corner of the separator who would cut ties on the sheafs or bundles and feed them into spinning flails and a series of flails screens, blowers that separated grain from the straw and expelled them into separate outlets. The later ones were fed by tossing the bundles into a wide trough with a belt running through the bottom that fed the monster.

Good Old Days Gone By

THERE WAS ONE FARM operation that comes to my mind that I would like to tell you about, hog feeding. It was very different in the old days compared to how it is now. It makes me wonder why pigs seemed to do so well on some of the things they were fed. A great many farmers kept swill barrels that they dumped table scraps, dishwater (with the soap suds), and they added a portion of ground feed. The ground feed could be wheat which they called middlens, along with a few ears of corn. I guess the lye in the homemade soap took care of any foreign things or bacteria in the slop or swill. Well, my brother Burt and I were a bit light to carry 12-quart buckets of swill. So Dad made us a wheelbarrow that held two buckets of swill. It surely was a dandy help, as the hog pen was about 300 yards from the well and was about 350 yards from the granary, and the footpath through the orchard to the pigpen was lined with poison ivy. Fortunately, Burt and I were immune to the damned stuff.

One of the hazards of feeding pigs with that dishwater mixture was some folks left toothpicks to get mixed in with that delightful slop. One time, Burt and I were butchering a couple of pigs for a neighbor when we found an intestine clogged with toothpicks. It was a good thing the pig was butchered when it was or it surely would have suffered a lot. Nowadays, some pigs never get their feet on the ground and are fed scientifically with sterile food.

That is my pig *tale*. But that's not quite all the things that deserve to be said about it. Us great over egotistical humans, or at least many of us, at some time or other, have used the name *pig* to describe a filthy person or thing. But that is not really a proper description of a pig. Pigs are one of the cleaner species of the animal kingdom if given their total freedom. They are much cleaner than some humans, and that's a fact! They are very smart animals, very good pets, but independent as hell. Now that is the end of my pig tale.

Remember the old-time circuses? Well, seems like they're mostly disappearing, so of course, that put a lot of people out of work. I'm not sure what they do with the animals when the circuses go under, but the clowns should not have any problems getting employment. If the trend keeps up, seems like the voters of this country have been sending about every clown they can get hold of to Washington, DC, to run things. And those old clowns have surely given a good performance at being funny. They have the best union there is because, over the years, the voters have let them run amok. When a senator or congressman's wife wants a new coat, they just raise their wages, and of course, they give the president's wages a boost also to keep him happy.

Then on top of that great act, they have a free benefit for everything anybody ever heard of. And after all that, they vote tax cuts to take care of the wealthy because most of those clowns say that's the way to keep the economy alive even if they have to dig deeper into social security and cut the school's budgets. Well, you younger folks think about that, and if I'm wrong, just mark this old farts *gab* as just that and have a happy life!

Now about my first experiences with horses. Dad bought Burt and I a Shetland pony named Buster. He was black and as gentle as could be but had a cute habit of playing a trick on whoever was first to ride him in the morning. He would gallop along real nice until he decided to play his trick. He never gave any warning and would slide to a stop and the rider would make a perfect dive over his head and land in front of him on the ground or dirt road. He never took another step while you were lying on the ground, but he would put his head down and nuzzle your face like he was showing his love for you and saying he was sorry.

The second was a bay mare named Nellie and one of the few extra good honest workhorses. She seemed to like to work, and if the horse that was hitched beside her was lagging and not pulling its own side, even she would reach over and bite it on the neck. She raised three beautiful colts for us in the five years that I had her.

Next was Bess, a chestnut-colored Belgian mare. She was likely the largest horse that I ever had and a very proud animal. She was very gentle and a willing worker, always pulling her share of a load. I think she was the best horse that I ever followed after with an old walking plow, and I have followed one of those things a good many hours in my younger years. She would walk up to a fence and turn and go right back in the furrow as that was the side she liked because she was the largest of the team. I never had to talk to her or drive her in any way; she just seemed to know what her job was.

The fourth was Nancy, the family pet. She was a mighty little mare, weighing about a thousand pounds and the most powerful little horse that I've ever seen. She was a really interesting animal, just full of surprises. She was a western cow pony with a Bar CJ brand on her hip. She was a pretty black-and-white pinto mustang. Nancy was like most of us Joneses; she was kind and gentle but had quite a temper when abused or treated badly. When Archer Jr. was five years old, I found him standing in Nancy's stall with his arms around her hind leg with his head against her knee hugging her. She had her head turned around, looking at him like he was her baby.

She was gentle with all the kids, but if Uncle Dave, who had not treated her very kindly, stepped in the door to feed his horse, she would get ugly and try to kick the heck out of anything near her. Archer Jr. likes to ride her while I cultivated the garden and potato patch with her. He straddled her back and held on to the harness. I did a great many things with Nancy's help. She moved our little three-room house four hundred feet from one side of our lot to the other side by pulling a pulley fourteen feet at a time. That was the length of the cable block, then we had to reset three in-line anchor posts and move plank skids and rollers. It took half an hour or more just to reset all that. George Davis and Charlie Sheldon helped with that and Charlie helped me one day after we got the house moved, getting it raised up to get the cellar wall under it.

Then there was Nellie, a sorrel with a white face. She was six years old when I got her and gentle but had never been broken to work. She was a beautiful animal but afraid to go through a doorway. One day, I had a problem with her going into the barn, and Fanny came out to help me. I gave Fanny the lead rope, and she got inside and tried to lead Nellie in, but I am not sure if the animal was afraid or just stubborn, but she wouldn't move. Fanny put the rope through a space back of a two-by-four and wrapped it around her hand. Well, Nellie reared up and pulled Fanny's hand into that opening and bruised it real bad. That was the only bad experience we ever had with Nellie. I sold her for a slight gain over what I had paid for her. She was the last horse we ever owned. We bought a Farmall tractor in 1949. I will always have a place in my heart for those wonderful friends although most people call them beasts of burden.

Just a few observations through a couple of real old eyes

I am just wondering if the common people like me are making any headway in the world these days. In the olden days, we always got enough exercise and got tired from working, so we were glad to sit down and get comfortable and happy to get a little rest. But it seems like with these wonderful computers and other such gadgets that folks get all tensed up about do the same things that a little bit of productive work did for us in the past. I guess that is what's called progress.

Now I'm not saying that the computer is not a great invention. But I will say that they are an awful nuisance sometimes if a fella is in a hurry and just about to wet his pants at a store checkout and that damned machine takes its time to go through its gyrations to tell the clerk the price of an item. And not only that, but I understand they can catch a virus from as far away as anywhere in the world. They say even a little kid could cause havoc or start trouble anywhere in the world just playing around with one of those critters. That's putting things way out of my league.

Another thing that is just a bit annoying to me is these credit cards. Seems like money isn't being used much anymore by a lot of people. Now I'm not saying that it's wrong to use a credit card if used in a sensible way, but a great many folks make a fool of themselves and make a nuisance to other folks with the little plastic things. I know of a lot of people get themselves so deep in debt with them that they keep themselves broke with no chance of ever getting out without help. And it's disturbing to be in the back of some dip who pays for a dime item with a card and then has to wait for a computer to approve and record the sale, and then the dip is taking time putting the damned thing back in a purse or wallet. It sure is progress.

Well, as long as I'm in this griping mood, I want to mention the topic of sports. The price of going to a game has gotten out of reach for the blue-collar workers. The multimillion-dollar contracts that are asked for and given to a great many players by their billion-dollar owners so they can take big tax write-offs that they can take through dirty tax loopholes that our great lawyer politicians have concocted is ruining the game. And radio and TV coverage runs so many commercials to be able to buy the broadcasting that it spoils the pleasure of hearing or watching the games at home. I see what used to be sports as just big business now. Well, that's enough gripes for now, but as time goes on, I'll have more of these old man's feebleminded things to bitch about. No offense intended to unguilty folks!

Some Thoughts

THE MOST PRIZED POSSESSIONS that I have had in my life are the people that I have in my family and my friends. I have been blessed with the world's best of both. I want to mention a few incidents that come to mind as they appear in this foggy head of mine. Not necessarily in the order that they happened in these past ninety-one years.

Our military family goes back to Granddad John W. Kennedy in the civil war. Archer, Jack, and Jim in the Army, Bob in the Air Force, Betty in the Air Force Auxiliary, sons-in-laws Bruce, Steve, and Carl in the Army, Jack in the Air Force, and daughter-in-law Dorothy in the Air Force. Also, grandchildren and great-grandchildren in the armed forces. I've just got to say I'm proud of all of them.

But it didn't seem like those guys in Congress thought very much about them when they sent them over there to Vietnam and have yet to call that bloodshed and killing anything but a police action. Our *policemen* have it a lot better than those boys did over there in that jungle and sand. I guess that I had better not say any more about this as every time I think of that bunch of clowns in Washington, my blood pressure soars.

I just think back to some of the ways good things happen in a fellow's lifetime. I just now thought of this as one of them.

I had known Cloyd Grimm from the time I was in school and several years in the fire department, then again when working for myself in the 1960s. One evening, Fanny and I went to the school for a baseball game. We were leaving to go home when we heard someone call our names; we turned to see who it was. In the many years we had known each other, Cloyd and us had just been speaking acquaintances, so we were surprised. We stopped and talked a couple

125

of minutes, and Cloyd said he wanted to say something that had been on his mind for some time. He said, "You know, we are getting older and I am wanting to be a friend before it gets too late for us older folks to be able to enjoy each other's company."

Fanny and I agreed that was a wonderful idea. So after that, we were able to enjoy many pleasant times together. After we moved to Florida, Cloyd and Bertha came to see us several times, and when we went back to Ohio, we always stopped in to see them. Many times since Cloyd has been gone, I've thought of his nice suggestion of friendship as an awfully good thing to remember.

I think of that story more each day now that I am a great-great-grandfather. Now when I go back home to Ohio, my old friends are no longer there. It's just a lonely experience. So my advice is to make friends as many and as long as you can. I've had a few that meant more to me than all the gold in Fort Knox.

Phyllis   Betty and Bob

Archer   Jack   Frances

Kay   James

About the Author

M Y FATHER WAS A very good storyteller about things that happened in the past, and at the urging of his grandson, Mike, he
began this autobiography. He was in his late eighties when he began.
It started by tape recording, but he was not comfortable with that
method, so he began handwriting stories and sending from Florida
to me in Ohio, then progressed to typewriting. I entered them into
my computer, inserting photos where they pertained to his writing.
This went on until he moved to Ohio where he passed away in 2007
at the age of ninety-seven.